MAKING
SPIRITUAL
SENSE

MAKING
SPIRITUAL
SENSE

CHRISTIAN
LEADERS
AS SPIRITUAL
INTERPRETERS

SCOTT CORMODE

WIPF & STOCK · Eugene, Oregon

Wipf and Stock Publishers
199 W 8th Ave, Suite 3
Eugene, OR 97401

Making Spiritual Sense
Christian Leaders as Spiritual Interpreters
By Cormode, D. Scott
Copyright©2006 by Cormode, D. Scott
ISBN 13: 978-1-62032-801-9
Publication date 1/1/2013
Previously published by Abingdon, 2006

CONTENTS

ACKNOWLEDGMENTS

Perhaps the loveliest task in writing a book is expressing gratitude to all those whose gifts made the endeavor possible. My formation as a scholar began at Yale University where I had the good fortune to work with Jon Butler and Skip Stout, who together convinced me to write in simple, straightforward sentences. While at Yale, I stumbled one day into the Program on Non-Profit Organizations (PONPO) and their project on religious institutions. At PONPO, Peter Dobkin Hall argued with me (and I mean that in the most complimentary way possible, Peter), Rhys Williams introduced me to the idea of cultural resources, and Lisa Berlinger walked me through the literature of Organizational Behavior (and especially Chris Argyris). The conversations I began at Yale continue on every page of this book.

In 1996, I came to the Claremont School of Theology. After Yale, I was all set to be a religious historian. I applied for thirteen history jobs and what I called "that quirky job at Claremont," which was the George Butler Chair in Church Administration and Finance. I will always be grateful for the freedom that the school gave me to invent my way into the position. At Claremont, I have learned much from Jack Fitzmier, Bob Edgar, Marjorie Suchocki, Elizabeth Conde-Frazier, Karen Dalton, Marvin Sweeney, and the rest of my faculty colleagues.

When I got the job teaching leadership to seminary students, I desperately needed dialogue partners. The Lilly Endowment, Inc., was kind enough to provide a grant to cultivate others who teach and write about Christian leadership. Over the years that grant has made wondrous things possible. It has allowed us to produce a website (www.christianleaders.org), to create a "community of practice" called the Academy of Religious Leadership (ARL), and to start a journal called the *Journal of Religious Leadership* (www.arl-jrl.org). The grant brought some magnificent dialogue partners into my world. I am especially grateful for people like Michael Jinkins, Craig Van Gelder, David Forney, Tom Tumblin, Mary Hess, and the host of scholars who have worked so hard on our mutual endeavor. I remain profoundly grateful to the Lilly Endowment for their support.

The actual writing of this book took place during a sabbatical year spent at the Princeton University Center for the Study of Religion. The weekly seminar hosted there by Robert Wuthnow provided a tremendous forum for experimenting with ideas. I also learned much from interacting with folks at Princeton Theological Seminary, especially Gordon Mikoski, Jack Stewart, Kenda Dean, and Rick Osmer.

A number of friends have been particularly important in providing feedback. Becky Bane has been a doctoral student, collaborator, and friend for many years. Many of the ideas in this book first came out in conversations with her. Emily Click has also taught me much. It is hard to explain all that I have learned from our years of conversations about leadership, life, and learning. There is simply too much to be cataloged. But I remain grateful for those lessons indeed. Likewise, Steve Davis has been a great friend and mentor, guiding me by his words and inspiring me with his example.

The last word, however, goes to my family. My parents—Dan and Ann—first introduced me to the themes of this book at the dinner table, when they taught me to see all of life in Christian terms. My children—Donley and Elizabeth—inspire me with their bright-eyed love. (Thanks, Elizabeth, for the copyediting.) And, of course, my wife—Genie—is most important of all. Her partnership and love remain God's greatest gift to me. I have been truly blessed.

Each of the people mentioned here has made this book better, yet none of them bears the responsibility for the errors or mistakes that lie within. Those are mine alone.

INTRODUCTION

From the earliest biblical times, God has called leaders to speak in God's name to God's people. These leaders provided a divine perspective on the daily dilemmas that the people faced. Moses, for instance, proclaimed to the people in Egypt that God had heard their cries. And then at Sinai, he gave them the law as a framework for interpreting life as God's chosen people. And, finally, as he prepared to hand leadership over to Joshua, Moses told the people who stood on the banks of the Jordan River that they had a choice between life in the land God promised and death in fearful wandering—and he urged them to choose life. At each of these critical moments in Hebrew history, God's appointed leader explained the spiritual meaning of the people's common experience.

This interpretative leadership continued once the people had taken possession of the land. There the judges reminded the people that their only hope lay in the God who brought them out of Egypt and not in being like other nations. This leadership culminated in Samuel's counsel that they would one day regret clamoring for a king. Yet God gave them a king. But Yahweh did not make the king the only leader of God's people. The prophets explained God's interpretation of national events to succeeding generations and instructed the kings when they strayed. Nathan, for example, helped David see his sin for what it was. Elijah and Elisha told the people that a wicked king was no reason to turn to false gods who would only let them down. Jeremiah informed the people of God's coming judgment and led them in lament when that judgment came crashing upon them. And Haggai called on the returning exiles to stop focusing on their own selfish pursuits long enough to rebuild God's temple. In each case, God's leader provided a divine perspective for God's people—a perspective that demanded action from those with ears to hear.

Likewise, in the New Testament, we see leaders whose primary task was to proclaim a new way of interpreting the world. Jesus repeatedly re-framed the very meaning of the law. For example, he said, "Let him who has no sin cast the first stone"—and punctured the self-righteous arrogance of a crowd that could no longer see its own sin. He also extended the law in new and uncomfortable ways, using for example the story of the Good Samaritan to show that "love thy neighbor" extends beyond the comfortable confines of polite society. After Jesus, the apostles sent epistle after epistle to newly formed churches in order to help them understand how Christians should interpret Greek culture. Should Christians purchase meat that had been sacrificed to idols? Did Christians in Europe and Asia Minor bear a responsibility for the poor in Jerusalem? These are the kinds of questions the apostles addressed. God called these people as leaders so that they would teach the church how to use Christian categories to make sense of their daily lives. Indeed, this act of interpretation was the primary way that the apostles and prophets led the people of God.

This work of interpretative leadership functioned at two levels. On the one hand, the apostles directed specific churches on how to handle specific circumstances. Indeed, the book of Philemon is all about adjudicating one such dilemma. But the Epistles also provide guidelines that allow the fledgling congregations to make their own decisions apart from the apostles. Even in Philemon, the Apostle Paul gives explanations that go far beyond the specific situation at hand. For example, he explains that Onesimus's identity as a brother in Christ is more important than his secular identity as Philemon's slave. Thus, the apostle's argument turns on a point that has broad application: one's identity in Christ transforms even the most basic relationships and ways of understanding a person. By interpreting the daily dilemmas of life, these Christian leaders inculcated basic principles that the church could apply to all of life.

We tend to forget, in this day of bureaucratic organizations and non-directive therapy, that the first duty of a Christian leader is to provide a Christian perspective, an interpretative framework for people who want to live faithful lives. We expect Christian leaders either to be hierarchical authorities that control their congregations or egalitarian enablers who support their staffs. And we call that leadership. But the authoritarians cannot mobilize God's people (at least not for long), and the enablers are ultimately ineffectual. We settle for these poor shadows of the leadership we see in the secular world. And we tend to forget that Christian

> The first duty of a Christian leader is to provide a Christian perspective, an interpretative framework for people who want to live faithful lives.

leadership is fundamentally an act of theological interpretation.

I want to argue for a different way to understand Christian leadership, one that says that the purpose of Christian leadership is to make spiritual meaning. Just as the prophets showed the Hebrews where God was at work in their world, so a Christian leader should help God's people see how to interpret their daily lives from God's perspective. And just as the Apostle Paul reinterpreted such basic tasks as buying meat to eat, so a Christian leader today leads by shaping the ways that God's people interpret everything going on in their worlds.

The stereotype of a leader is a person who tells people what to do. But the best leaders rarely have to order people around. Instead, the best leaders give people the tools to think for themselves. And then those leaders point people on a path forged by those new ideas. That's what Martin Luther King did when he awoke America—white and black—to civil rights. And that's what Jesus did when he preached the Sermon on the Mount. The best leaders change the way that we see the world.

What does that look like in a local congregation? There was once a congregational board of elders discussing the question of money. Most of the conversation focused on the fear they had because there never seemed to be enough money. The elders were looking for a program that would increase funds. In other words, they wanted a leader who would tell them what to do. But that's not what they needed from a leader. In fact, every time the congregation raised a little money, the board spent it, almost immediately, because there were lots of pressing needs. What they eventually came to see was that the key issue was not the amount of money. The key issue was fear. They only saw the world in terms of scarcity—and, of course, that meant that they were always afraid. They did not need someone to tell them what to do. They needed someone to help them see the world differently. Their leader talked with them one night about some insights from the biblical scholar, Walter Brueggemann, who uses the Old Testament to show how we can replace our "myths of scarcity" with "liturgies of abundance."[1] And eventually this church board began to discuss ways of reshaping its outlook so that it focused on God's abundance. It took a number of months of work and a lot of trial and error before they had conquered their fears. And it would be easy to say that those months of work represented the place of "leadership." But that would miss the lesson this story has to tell. The key moment was when the board turned from scarcity and toward abundance. And the most important moment of leadership happened when their leader helped them see their world differently. Everything else flowed from that moment when the elders adopted a new way of seeing the world—one built on abundance rather than scarcity.

It is easy to misunderstand leadership as telling people what to do. And it's not even about telling them what to think because, as we'll see later, no leader can do that for someone else. You cannot coerce people. But a leader can entice people to change what we will call their "mental models"—the categories (like scarcity) they use to interpret their worlds. And when people have new mental models, they can make spiritual sense for themselves. That's what it means to lead the People of God.

There are three components to this book. Part 1 looks at the process by which a person makes sense of her own life. Why is it, for instance, that the Lord of All Life is relevant to some aspects of most parishioners' lives, but off-limits to other parts? The answer has to do with how people make meaning. Making meaning happens all the time. Every time you or I encounter some new situation we have to figure what the situation means and what parts of it are most important. This process is crucial to leadership, yet it is rarely discussed. We will examine it in detail so that we know what people hear and how they make meaning. Once we understand this meaning-making process, we can show how leaders can shape that meaning so that people adopt a Christian perspective on their worlds.

Part 2 will show how shaping meaning allows pastors to guide their congregations. In other words, it explains how making spiritual meaning is leadership. It describes a collection of "cultural resources." We are used to thinking of resources as tangible things like buildings and funds. And we all know that it is hard to mobilize a congregation without resources. But this part shows that there are other resources that are far more important—resources like beliefs, stories, and values. A meaning-making leader can, as we shall see, mobilize these resources to transform a congregation.

Surrounding these two parts is a frame, the third component of the book. The introduction and the conclusion look at one particularly troublesome question—the question of money—to illustrate the importance of making spiritual meaning. The rest of this introduction explains how the money question is entangled with some of the most difficult questions that face the contemporary church. The conclusion illustrates how the book's central ideas might help a pastor to address this vexing issue.

Every Christian leader will at some point have to face the money question. Most do it with tremendous ambivalence. Pastors don't like preaching about money and church boards don't like having to balance the budget. Yet money remains an important topic. And it keeps getting harder to come by. Giving within my own (Presbyterian) denomination, for instance, has dropped to a fraction of what it was a generation ago. It is not surprising, then, to hear church leaders talk about the monetary crisis that our churches face.

What is surprising is the reason for the crisis. Denominational leaders have for years claimed that the crisis stemmed from factors beyond their control. Some called it a backlash against a principled stance on civil rights.[2] Others blamed sociodemographic categories like the facts that women were entering the workforce and baby boomers were having fewer babies. And a few simply claim that the selfishness of consumer culture is winning out. But these theories amount to little more than defensive reasoning. The problem with the claims is not that they are wrong; it's that they are not useful.[3] Women may be working, but they are not the source of our problems. Denominations did take a principled stand on civil rights, but that did not alienate a generation of Americans as these leaders claim. The root of the crisis, according to the most sophisticated scholarship on American religion, is pastors like you and me. "The current financial crisis is, in fact, a *spiritual crisis*," researcher Robert Wuthnow discovered. "The problem lies less in parishioners' pocketbooks than in their hearts and less in churches' budgets than in clergy's understanding of . . . their members' lives."[4] The crisis exists because the people who speak for God have not provided a Christian perspective on the issues that matter most to the people of God. Let me be clear. Neither Wuthnow nor I have any interest in blaming clergy. The goal instead is to name a dilemma that pastors like you and me regularly face as we minister to God's people.

Wuthnow interviewed pastors and listened to laypeople talk about money. He found that clergy could talk about the plight of the poor and could pray for the needy across the sea. But these same ministers were surprisingly inarticulate when describing the everyday lives of their own parishioners. Ministers were more likely to talk about symbolic issues like funding for the National Endowment for the Arts than they were to address the pressures their own members experience at work and at home. Wuthnow found that lay "people are much more concerned about how to work responsibly" than they are about the latest volley in the culture wars. The lay leaders he interviewed told him that they wanted their churches to help them know how to understand the worlds of work and money from a faith perspective. Thus, he concluded, "The clergy must do a better job of relating theology to everyday life."[5] Helping pastors figure out how to make that connection is a significant goal of this book.

Money is, of course, only the tip of the iceberg. There are a host of related issues that characterize the lives that most church members lead. Wuthnow heard people talk about the pressures that weigh on families—"pressures of working harder to make ends meet, worries about retaining one's job, lack of time for one's self and one's family, marital strains associated with two-career households, and the incessant demands of advertising and the marketplace."[6] *Time* magazine documented these concerns with a pair of insightful articles in the mid-1990s. One article started out rather optimistically. "In every way that can be measured," the magazine reported, "Americans are living much better than" they did in the 1970s.[7] People own more things and enjoy more luxuries. But the article documents a more ominous trend as well. People also feel far more insecurity. One woman talked about a mortgage, car payments, credit card debt, and wanting to "help with college for the kids." She confessed, "I worry a lot about what's going to happen." Americans may have more stuff, but they are a lot more fearful too. And fear is a deeply spiritual category, one that cries out for theological interpretation.

Unfortunately, the theological categories we have learned do not help us address this fear. Sermons tend either to scold people for their vainglorious ways or to dismiss their fears by telling them to "consider the lilies of the field." But the *Time* article makes it hard to justify either of those interpretations. "Rising standards of living, to many, mean largely an increase in the number of things they 'must' buy." And just when we think that we have heard this story, the magazine says more. "This is not just crass materialism; many of the new musts are not goods but services—medical insurance, day care for young children, college tuition for teenagers—which have rocketed in price." The sermon on vainglorious accumulation will not work because no one is going to say college is a luxury item or that medical insurance is just another way to indulge the baser instincts. And Wuthnow's clergy are not sure what to say about the fact that, according to *Time*, "so many people feel they are working harder and harder just to keep up."[8] We need better categories for interpreting money and material things.

A companion article in *Time* told a similar story without the big statistics. It documented the life of a single mother who was living with these pressures.[9] Lori is in her midthirties and has a one-year-old son named Sam. She owns her own home and manages an auto repair shop. Time is as important to her as money. "The week before Sam was born," she says, "I washed every piece of clothing there was, including what I was wearing," and ruefully concludes, "That was the last time the laundry was caught up." She's been racing ever since. "I used to be a list maker . . . And now I don't even have time to make lists." That's why she admits, "Some nights I could scream and cry and have a nervous breakdown." There are just too many concerns to juggle. Lori's mother, Doris, cares for Sam during the days, giving up her retirement years because, as the article reports, "she thought about what matters to her most, [saying] 'I knew it would make me tired . . . but what's more important than my grandson?'" Doris worries not only for her daughter and grandson, she also frets about her own mother, who resides in a nursing home. These are the pressures that Wuthnow found to be common among the people who belong to our churches. And these are the concerns that demand spiritual meaning.

These are, unfortunately, exactly the topics about which American clergy have surprisingly little to say, according to the pastors that Wuthnow interviewed. "Faced with this dilemma" of mounting pressures on their time and money, Wuthnow found, Americans turn "in large numbers to the churches to find help. Yet the churches don't seem to be making much of a difference."[10] The pastors that Wuthnow interviewed reported that they are not sure what to say, so they avoid the uncomfortable topic of money as much as possible.

Why then do clergy have so little to say about money? One problem is that the interpretations pastors have learned over the years do not help them understand and interpret Lori's life. The dominant interpretations about money involve *condemning materialism* and *scolding selfishness*—stories that we have already established don't apply to worries about college tuition, health insurance, and nursing home care. But the interpretations carry tremendous weight, if only because there are no other categories for interpreting money issues.

Let me illustrate how powerful these standard interpretations are. In a course I teach on Church Leadership, I have students read Wuthnow's study and the *Time* articles. We discuss Lori's dilemma together. And we spend considerable time talking in class about the quotation that says, "this is not just crass materialism." I tell them that one of the questions on the midterm will ask them to come up with a theological interpretation for the pressures people experience—one that cannot resort to considering the lilies of the field. I remind the students on the exam paper that, "blaming parishioners for their materialism would be a wrong answer." Yet every year it seems there are students who begin their essays by rejecting the selfishness interpretation, but who end their essays blaming people for their fears. The standard interpretations are so strong that even people who reject them at the start of their essays end up advocating them. Pastors crave the basic categories for interpreting the things that keep people awake at night.

I believe, however, that we have to preach about money for the same reasons that we have to preach about raising kids—because God cares about the things that matter most. These are the worries that keep people awake at night, and thus the ones that demand theological interpretation.

What can this discussion of money teach us about Christian leadership? We learn that we cannot rely on threadbare interpretations if we are going honor the difficult choices that many of our parishioners face. We learn that we will need to construct new ways to talk about the difficult choices people need to make and the legitimate anxieties that they feel. And we will need to overcome the stigma attached to conversations about money. But there is something deeper we can learn about leadership as well. The answers that we have proposed so far may help us solve the problem of interpreting money, but they won't tell us why the problem exists in the first place. Those readers who simply want to answer the money question should skip ahead to the conclusion. I am playing here on Chris Argyris's distinction between double loop learning and single loop learning.[11] The purpose of single loop learning is to solve the problem at hand. But the purpose of double loop learning is to figure out why the problem came into being. His premise is that problems are the product of the organizational environment. So, to return to our current example, Argyris would ask what the existence of this problem teaches us about our congregations and the pastors who lead them.

Pastors have such a difficult time talking about money because two important forces in American religion converge on them at once when the topic of money comes up. First, the standard interpretations no longer work. So ministers have to come up with their own interpretations. And that's where the second force becomes important. Clergy have a very difficult time creating new interpretations when one has not already been established for them. Yet, like Moses and Paul before them, God calls Christian leaders to lead by speaking new meaning into difficult and confusing situations.

One final example may explain why this process of meaning making is so important. We might call it the "new parents problem." We have all known pregnant couples that proudly proclaim that they are going to be different than their parents were. They often focus on one characteristic behavior and tell everyone why their parents had it all wrong. My wife and I had one friend—an expectant father we'll call Doug—who described in detail why yelling at children does not help anyone. It frustrates the child, he said, and does not even get the point across because the child stops listening. Doug could explain all that was wrong with the parenting style he learned from his parents. We have all known people like that. And we all know how the story ends. Years later, Doug was yelling at his son just as his parents yelled at him. When I teased him about his boastful claim that he would never yell at his children, he was incredulous. "I would never have said such a thing."[12]

There is an important lesson here. Doug discredited an old behavior (yelling) without creating a new way of being to replace it. So when he became angry and frustrated, he only had one resource to draw on. He did not have any other options, so he returned to old behavior even though he could explain in detail why it was wrong. He did not know any other way. The same thing happened to my students who ended up condemning the materialism of wanting basic necessities like health insurance and elder care. They did not know any other way to talk about money. So, when they felt the pressure of the moment, they returned to the only interpretation they knew—even though they could explain in detail why the interpretation was inappropriate. The lesson, then, is this. It is not enough to discredit non-Christian interpretations of the world. We have to build Christian ways of making sense of daily life that will replace them. But the good news is that once God's people internalize the Christian way of seeing the world, it will take a great effort to dislodge it.

All this makes it particularly important to understand how people make meaning when they encounter new situations. That is the focus of the next part.

Notes

1. Walter Brueggemann, *Deep Memory, Exuberant Hope: Contested Truth in a Post-Christian World* (Minneapolis: Fortress Press, 2000).

2. For one example of how entrenched some denominational leaders can be in denial of their own complicity, see my "A Financial History of Congregations since World War II" in *The Organizational Revolution: Presbyterians and American Denominationalism*, ed. by Milton J. Coalter, John M. Mulder, and Louis B. Weeks (Louisville: Westminster/John Knox Press, 1992). The article specifically examined the conventional wisdom that the denomination's principled support of Angela Davis in 1970 precipitated the financial crisis. The article shows that the trend started in 1963, which means that its cause could not be something that happened seven years later. When I presented this material to denominational leaders, they told me that my data must be wrong. I assured them that the data came from their own records. At that point one bureaucrat said, "Then our data must be wrong because we know what happened." The cost of exploring other sources for the problem was too high for this powerful denominational leader to acknowledge relatively simple facts. He thus retreated to what Chris Argyris calls "defensive reasoning," Argyris, "Skilled Incompetence," *Harvard Business Review* (September-October 1986): 2–7.

3. Argyris, "Teaching Smart People How to Learn," *Harvard Business Review* (May-June 1991): 8–9.

4. Robert Wuthnow, *The Crisis in the Churches: Spiritual Malaise, Fiscal Woe* (New York: Oxford University Press, 1997), 5. The book is summarized in article form as Robert Wuthnow, "The Crisis in the Churches" in *Financing American Religion* ed. by Mark Chaves and Sharon L. Miller (Walnut Creek, Calif.: AltaMira Press, 1999), 67–78 and in editorial form as Wuthnow, "Churches' Financial Woes: A Crisis of the Spirit," *The Chronicle of Philanthropy* (October 2, 1997): 4–5.

5. Wuthnow, "Crisis in the Churches," in Chaves & Miller, *Financing American Religion*, 74.

6. Wuthnow, *Crisis in the Churches: Spiritual Malaise, Fiscal Woe*, 6.

7. George J. Church, "Are We Better Off?" *Time* 147, no. 5 (January 29, 1996); cf. Nancy Gibbs and Michael Duffy, "Desperately Seeking Lori," *Time* 148, no. 18 (October 14, 1996).

8. Church, "Are We Better Off?"

9. Gibbs and Duffy, "Desperately Seeking Lori."

10. Wuthnow, "Crisis in the Churches," in Chaves and Miller, *Financing American Religion*, 71.

11. Argyris, "Double Loop Learning in Organizations," *Harvard Business Review* (September-October 1977): 115–24; cf. Argyris, "Double Loop Learning, Teaching, and Research," *Academy of Management Learning and Education* 1, no. 2 (2002): 206–18.

12. This and many other examples in this book have been modified in fundamental ways to protect the identities of the individuals involved and to make the examples more readable.

PART ONE

MAKING SENSE
OF NEW SITUATIONS

A cryptic phone call from Laura Webber told Rev. Charlotte Robinson that something strange was afoot. Charlotte, the pastor of the First Presbyterian Church of Almond Springs, California, took the message off the answering machine one afternoon after her secretary, Mavis, had left. Laura was perhaps Charlotte's closest friend in town and she did not sound at all like herself in the message. Her usually confident manner had become brittle and seething.[1]

"I heard Old Man Rivers is coming to see you," the message began bitterly. "Don't let him do it. It's not right." There was a hint of threat in Laura's voice. The pastor asked herself, "What's going on?" She wondered who her friend could mean. *The only Rivers I know,* " Charlotte thought, *"is a guy named Gary Rivers who's visited the church a couple of times. I need to figure out what is going on.*" She was reaching for the phone to call Laura when there was a tentative knock on the outer office door.

"Hello, Mr. Rivers," Charlotte said.

"Please call me Gary," the man answered in a slow, sonorous voice. Charlotte guessed he was about her own age. *"And that,"* the forty-three-year-old pastor thought silently, *"does not make him an old man."* He seemed shy and ill at ease. His eyes frequently flashed toward the door as if someone else was coming.

He filled Charlotte in on his history, "I grew up in Almond Springs but then, umm . . . well," another glance at the door, "I left about fifteen years ago. Now I have come back to town to care for my old man. How's that for irony?" There was shame on his face, mixed with confusion. Charlotte wondered what Old Man Rivers could have done to cause Gary such pain.

"I am not sure I should be coming to church after what the Old Man did," he said after a moment. "But I met a man once who said that the church should be the first place to forgive. And I been thinking a lot about that." He had the manner of a man resigned to his fate.

"'We are in the forgiving business;' that's what a friend of mine likes to say," Charlotte remarked brightly, wondering where Gary was going.

"Yeah, I hope so," he said, almost to himself, "because that's what I need . . . forgiving."

Charlotte was confused again. "Why do you need forgiving?" she asked.

There was another knock on the inner office door before he could answer. It was Doc Davis, perhaps the wisest member of her church. "Can I schedule you for later?" Charlotte asked discreetly, wanting to get back to Gary.

"No. You don't understand, pastor," Doc said with a smile, "I am the one who called to say I was bringing this young man to see you. I'm sorry I am late. I had an unexpected patient who thought she had the measles. It was only an allergy."

Gary called to him from inside. "I thought you told her I was coming, Doc."

The old physician stepped through the door and turned to the young man, "Of course, I made the appointment earlier today."

"But, Doc," Gary said plaintively, "she just asked me why the Old Man needs forgiving."

"Why don't you just tell her exactly what you told me," Doc said, closing the door and sitting next to Gary.

"I got the nickname Old Man in high school. All the football players gave each other names like we were a motorcycle gang or fighter pilots. Like Walt Webber, he was Wild One. We thought we were so tough. Anyway, my name stuck. It used to be that everyone in town called me Old Man, even at church. Me and the guys we'd hang out together after work, even when we were all married. Some of the guys started drinking a lot, especially Walt. Laura tried to get him to stop after they married, but he was a bull. You couldn't tell him nothing. And he had a temper. He started knocking Laura around when he was drunk. We tried to stop him, me and my wife Sally. But there was not much we could do." Gary was quiet for a moment before continuing. Charlotte felt empathy for Gary's obvious brokenness and was already worried about where the story was headed. Gary looked at his feet as he went on.

"I never touched Sally. Then one night . . . I got mad and smacked her. Everyone thought her daddy did it—until she divorced me and moved away. Then not long afterward, Walt and Laura had their thing. And, well, everyone blamed me for Sally and for Laura." He paused, waiting for a reaction. He still had not looked at Charlotte since he started describing his earlier life. Charlotte did not yet understand exactly what Gary was feeling but she was getting closer to the reason he had come. She wanted to ask him why everyone blamed him for what happened with Laura, but Doc jumped in before she could speak, "Tell her the rest of the story. Tell her what you told me."

"I can't blame Walt or the alcohol. It's all my fault. I could have been arrested. Yeah, I should have been arrested. A month or so after Sally left me, I just couldn't take it any more. I decided just to run away from Almond Springs. I moved to Oklahoma and worked oil for a spell. And then I did some other stuff. I was lonely and scared. I was scared to drink and scared to date. I did not have a drink for about five years after I left town. I did not go out on a date until two years ago. I figured that I did it once and I might do it again." Charlotte had never seen someone so totally ashamed of himself. A psalm flashed through her mind, "A broken and contrite heart the Lord will not despise."

"I was especially afraid to go to church," Gary said, looking up for the first time at the pastor. "But then in Oklahoma I started going to a Sunday night church. It was a Christian Missionaries Alliance church, I think they called it. They didn't know what I had done. So I started praying with them. And then every time I moved I tried to go to a church. At one of the churches, I told the minister about all I'd done and he told me that Old Man Rivers was dead and that in the Bible it says I can be a new creation. I stenciled those words on the back of my tool chest. 'New Creation.' I haven't wanted anyone to call me Old Man since then—just Gary." Charlotte's mind raced as he spoke. She had to restrain herself to keep from interrupting him. *"What this poor man needs,"* Charlotte thought as he continued, *"is to know that God has forgiven him."*

"Now I had to come home to Almond Springs. My father is sick and someone has to look after him to see that he doesn't fall and that he eats right. I been here since summer but did not really come to church until Doc told me it was OK. He told me I should come talk to you because you would understand even though you're a woman and all." He paused for a moment. Charlotte nodded and looked as kind as she could. Her heart ached for him but she waited to speak because he looked like he might have something else he wanted to get out.

"The real reason I came, though, is that I want to join the church. I've never actually belonged to a church, even when my family came here a long time ago. And Doc says it's time for me to be baptized, that it's part of that new creation thing." Then he shrugged and said, "So that's why I'm here."

"Let me say it again, Gary," Charlotte began. "The church is in the forgiving business," she put her hand softly on his knee, "God does not ask you to grovel and neither do we. God promises that once you have made your confession that God will separate your sin from you." They continued talking for some time. She told Gary about King David's sin, about Nathan the Prophet, and about God's ultimate blessing on David's union with Bathsheba.

Gary kept asking the same question again and again in different ways, not fully convinced that God could forgive him when he was not sure he could forgive himself. They talked until Gary finally felt ready to leave.

Doc Davis walked Gary out to his car and then came back inside to talk with Charlotte. "You did the right thing," he said. "But there are going to be some problems."

Charlotte felt that she had done the only thing a pastor could do. "Forgiveness is not mine to dispense," she said to Doc. "I can only point Gary to what God has already done. I know there are problems, but I don't understand them. I got a phone call from Laura Webber."

"I'll bet you did," Doc interjected.

"Why'd you tell her about the meeting?" Charlotte asked.

"I didn't," Doc said, "I'd bet it was Mavis, your secretary. She seemed quite incredulous when I called to set up the appointment." Mavis's indiscretion was an ongoing problem for Charlotte. But she put aside her concerns about Mavis so that she could deal with the matter at hand.

"Why is Laura so upset?" Charlotte asked, "I hardly recognized her voice on the phone. She sounded so vindictive, almost hateful."

"I should probably tell you the whole story," Doc began. "You'll need to hear it if you are going to minister to everyone who needs your care in this situation." He paused. "Now, you know how I feel about Laura," he said looking directly at the pastor. Charlotte nodded. She knew that Doc regarded Laura almost as a daughter and that Laura revered him as a father figure. Indeed, Charlotte suspected that Doc's regard for Laura is what prompted him to tell the church it was acceptable to hire a woman as pastor.

"Laura married quite young, not long after her mother died (she never knew her father). She was still commuting to Fresno State University at the time. Walt Webber was a good old boy in a small town. He played football, drove a fast car, and married the most popular girl in Almond Springs. They had a son less than a year later."

It sounded to Charlotte like a story straight out of *American Graffiti*. But then, she thought after a moment, it was not all that different from her own suburban upbringing. She knew people like that. Only the scenery was different.

"But Walt drank . . . a lot," Doc continued. "And, like Gary Rivers said, Walt had a violent temper. I think things would have exploded much sooner if Gary and his wife Sally had not kept Walt in check. It started with open hand slaps, and there were times that he would scold her like a child. Then Sally divorced Gary and there was no one for Laura to call when she saw it coming."

Charlotte was aghast. The portrait did not match her friend at all. *"Laura's not the victim type,"* Charlotte caught herself thinking. And then she immediately scolded herself, wondering what it meant to think that anyone's personality type would make her or him a victim.

"One night in July, when Laura's son was about four, Walt came home drunk again. They argued and this time he punched her in the face. Knocked her out. When she came to, he was vomiting in the bathroom. She eventually pulled herself up and called the police. A young officer came out. And he reacted like Laura was his little sister." Doc shook his head in disgust.

"The cop took Walt outside and beat him senseless. Broke his arm in the process. Then he handcuffed him (broken arm and all) and took him to jail. The next day they called me to set his arm. Laura convinced the police to drop the domestic violence charges so long as Walt said nothing about how the fracture occurred. She took Walt home that afternoon and by dinnertime he was gone. He never again had anything to do with Laura, their son, or this town."

Charlotte ached for her friend. *"What a burden Laura must still carry,"* Charlotte thought. The pastor knew from Laura's voice on the phone that her wounds had not nearly healed. But she did not completely understand. From the phone call, Charlotte knew that Laura blamed

Gary. In fact, Gary seemed to think he was at fault as well. The question was why.

"Why did Gary Rivers take it so hard?" Charlotte asked.

Doc answered, "Word got around, of course, about what Walt had done. And with Walt gone, people took it out on Old Man Rivers. 'He'd been Walt's best friend,' they said around town. 'He should have stopped him. But instead the Old Man beat his wife and now look what's happened to our Laura.' It was unfair and it was cruel. One old woman stopped him on the street and scolded him up and down. She'd got the story confused and thought that he'd beat Laura. All most people knew was that Gary was a wife-beater and that Laura got beat up. It all kind of became one incident. That's just the way the story got told and repeated. And, with Walt gone, Gary was the only one left to blame. So Old Man Rivers left Almond Springs. And you know the story from there."

Charlotte felt ill, like someone watching a tape replay of a horrific car accident. There were so many old, hidden wounds opening again in her congregation.

"This is going to take some time," she thought, *"and it's going to be my job to get these people ready to hear God's message of hope."* But before she could do that, she knew that she had to hear the rest of Laura's story.

"How has this affected Laura?" she asked Doc, hoping to keep him talking.

"The lesson Laura took from this," he said slowly, "was that men are dangerous. Before that night, she thought of her husband and the police officer as good men. But for years afterward, she saw men (especially those near her age) as time bombs—potentially explosive and inherently dangerous. Enough time and a lot of therapy since then means that she knows that's not true, at least it's not supposed to be." Charlotte guessed that Laura's daughterly relationship with Doc had also helped to heal some of the wounds.

"All this seems to be at odds with the Laura I know," Charlotte wondered aloud.

"Oh, it's made her a different person," Doc began and then stopped himself. "Well, not a different person exactly. But she is always in complete control of her world now. She is the organizer, the leader, the one who tells everyone else what to do. Look at the way she dresses, always wearing elegant suits with silk blouses, never polyester." Charlotte understood what he meant.

"You're right," Charlotte said, "I think of her as regal. She carries herself like a queen."

"Exactly," Doc responded, "And look at the way the town has responded to her. No Almond Springs man would ever ask her on a date. They think too highly of her. They think she is out of their league. In fact, her son had trouble dating in high school because none of the girls wanted to be compared to 'the perfect mother.'" Charlotte marveled at how little she knew about her good friend.

"And that reputation buys Laura a lot in town," Doc continued. "You know that as the vice principal at Almond Springs High School, she is a great role model for the girls. They all want to be like her—to dress like her and have people treat them with such respect. She even does all the Sex Education classes for girls at the high school because the girls trust her. And she can say whatever she wants in those classes because the parents think she is above reproach. Small town reputations get exaggerated. They see her as someone who has elevated herself above her abuse—elevated herself from victim to role model."

Charlotte was beginning to see her friend in a new, more complicated, light. And she was also beginning to understand just how difficult Gary Rivers's returning was going to be for Laura. She turned to Doc: "Gary's reappearance has got to be really unsettling for her. Walt, Gary, and even Sally disappeared long before she was able to resolve her feelings toward them. Part of her probably feels very vulnerable."

"And she is not going to want to be a victim in public ever again," Doc said. "For Gary to find forgiveness, and for the town to accept him, he's going to have to make some kind of public declaration of repentance. There are all sorts of possibilities for a baptismal service that brings healing to the whole community. But for that to happen, Laura has to become the victim again. And she's not going to want any kind of public conversation that diminishes her role. There is no way that she wants the girls at the high school to think of her as anything less than the perfect role model. Perhaps I was too hasty in offering Gary such hope."

"No, Doc, you did the right thing," Charlotte answered. "If a church cannot proclaim forgiveness, we might as well go home. And I'd love to help Laura see—and those high school kids understand too—that God embraces us in our brokenness. Victim is the wrong term. We are all broken by sin, our sin and the sin of others. But the hope of the gospel is that God meets us in our brokenness. My hope for Laura is not that she will hide her hurts, but that she will bring them before God. No, Doc, you did the right thing. The question for us is how to help the town understand that it was the right thing, and that we all need to grow because of it."

Doc and Charlotte then prayed together. And they agreed not to tell anyone about their conversations until they had a chance to meet again. "If we are going to help this town grow spiritually through this," Charlotte concluded, "we are going to need a plan."

Meaning making happens simultaneously at more than one level. Think back on the story you just read, where Doc Davis brings a broken young man named Gary "Old Man" Rivers to see Rev. Charlotte Robinson. Rivers, you will recall, is there because he wishes to be baptized and to join the church, but he first wants to confess a fifteen-year-old sin that weighs on him. The complication, of course, is that any public confession of his sin will embarrass a prominent member of the church, Charlotte's friend Laura Webber. Even before Doc brings Gary to visit the pastor, Charlotte has to do her own interpretation. She is working to make sense of Laura's angry phone call. But before she can work too far into her own interpretation, Gary arrives and her interpretative duty shifts to helping the young man understand that his sin can be forgiven. He is not sure that God can forgive him when he cannot forgive himself. Much of the conversation is about Charlotte's attempts to understand Gary's dilemma and her desire to help him see that God can and will forgive him. But when Gary leaves, Charlotte and Doc take on a new interpretative task. They begin to wonder how they are going to help their congregation understand this situation. Thus, Charlotte finds herself working on at least three interpretative levels all at the same time. She has to manage her own meaning, she has to help Gary understand, and she has to think about the implications for her congregation. And, of course, the three levels (self, individual, and communal) will often be in tension with one another. What Gary most needs in order to understand God's love (i.e., to experience the catharsis of public confession and forgiveness) is exactly the thing that the pastor worries would open the most wounds in the community. If Charlotte is going to help her congregation understand this situation, she will need to understand for herself how people and groups make sense of new and difficult situations.

The pastor's long-term goal is to help people to discover and internalize a specific interpretative framework, one that will make it possible to see all of life from a distinctly Christian perspective. Over the course of this book, we will develop the tools we need to explain this internalized interpretative framework and show how this framework enables Christian leaders to lead God's people. A preview of the argument might go something like this:

1. People construct their own meaning when they make sense of situations.
2. Leadership is about making meaning.
3. Leadership arises from the mutual efforts of the people in the community to make meaning.
4. Finally, while the leader oversees the meaning-making process, he or she does not control it.

These points will, of course, grow in the pages that follow. And the first step in that direction is for us to understand more deeply how people make sense of new situations in their lives.

Every time that you or I encounter a new situation, we have to figure out how to make sense of it.[2] That happens because the new events we experience each day have no single, unambiguous meaning. We have to interpret them. We have to search the experiences we've had, the ideas we've heard, and the stories we've known.[3] We have to find some way to match the new situation with something familiar or we have to create new categories to make sense of it. But we cannot process the event until we've interpreted it. If we don't process it, we lose it—like a letter that never got filed or a computer file that never got saved.[4] Let me illustrate what it means to make sense of a new situation.

The other day I was walking through a crowded grocery store. I saw a young girl in a pink dress holding back tears. There was a clerk bent down next to her. All at once, the girl's face brightened and she ran to a man who held her tight. I put all the clues together and I smiled because a little lost girl had found her daddy. At least, I assume that's what happened. I'll never know for sure. I made all sorts of inferences in order to assemble my observations into a story. For example, I looked at the kneeling woman's green vest and nametag and I guessed that she was a clerk working at the store. I figured out that the girl's pinched face and watery eyes indicated distress. Indeed, I assumed that the girl held the man tightly

(I called it a "hug" in my mind) indicated an affectionate intimacy in their relationship. In other words, I am proficient enough in reading American society that I could take a five second scene and compose a story that made sense of it. I could smile because I "knew" the story had a happy ending. And I remember the scene because I had a label for it. I made sense of the situation; I knew what it meant.[5]

A few weeks before a different story had played out in front of me. In this case, I had never seen such a thing before. But I was still able to make sense of it. My car was sitting at a traffic light in my sleepy suburban town. It had to be a Thursday afternoon because I was listening to a Dodger game on the radio. That's when I heard sirens. All of a sudden three police cars converged on the intersection from different directions. The one coming from the east followed a small white sedan into a gas station parking lot. I did not think much of it until the officers in the car swung open their doors, drew their weapons, and pointed their guns at the sedan. Just then the police cruiser coming from the north did a power slide and skidded itself in front of the sedan. Its officer also drew his gun and crouched behind a door. Within seconds the third black-and-white arrived from the west. It stopped in the middle of the intersection. Its officer leaped out the door, ran to the trunk of his cruiser, and pulled out a submachine gun. He pointed it at the white car as the first officer shouted something. The occupants of the sedan gently raised both hands out of the car's side windows. Each occupant slowly exited the car, raised their arms, and walked toward the first set of policemen, who laid them on the ground and handcuffed them. Just then the stoplight in front of me turned green and, after a moment's hesitation to see if anyone would direct me, I turned left and drove back to my office. It all happened in the time it took a traffic light to cycle.

Again, my experience with the culture allowed me to draw a number of conclusions. For example, I instinctively assumed that the police were the good guys and that they had a reason to take these extraordinary measures.[6] I never felt in any danger. In the few seconds it took me to process the situation, it was clear to me that the "suspects" (as I called them in my mind) were surrendering (I assumed this because they put their hands in the air). I realized later that I was interpreting the situation based on what I'd seen in movies, not from any storehouse of personal knowledge. This suspect-surrendering episode looked liked the end of any number of television police shows. I was reassured because I "knew" we were at the end of the story—even though my only "experiences" had been with stories that were fictional and contrived. I did not consciously decide to relax. That's simply the way my body responded to seeing the suspects surrender. I'd made sense of the situation and signaled my body to breathe easily even before I had the words to explain what had happened.

But just a few changes in the details would have made this a terrifying story. What if three white sedans had stopped a police cruiser and surrounded it with drawn guns? All my assumptions about living safely under the protection of the law would (at least for the moment) have been called into question. What if one of the suspects had stepped out of the car, opened a trench coat, and revealed several sticks of dynamite? That's not how TV shows end. That's how the drama begins. Then I would have been afraid. The fearful surge of adrenaline would have come just as automatically as the relaxing breath I took when I saw the suspects surrendering. We make sense of situations in such a way that the name we give to the situation leads us naturally to a response in action.[7]

Most leaders tend to take this process of *sensemaking* for granted. It is just the way things are, they say. But I will argue that we need to pay greater attention to how people interpret their worlds. We know, for example, that people use spiritual categories to make sense of some aspects of life (e.g., the death of a loved one) but rarely use similar categories to describe other aspects (e.g., few people describe their job as a *calling*). Yet most pastors adhere to a theology that says no part of life is detached from God. We believe that every circumstance has theological meaning. Part of the pastoral role is to make that meaning clear.

There is an important leadership principle here. To the extent that Christian leaders provide people with a theological framework for action, they are proclaiming God's message of love and justice. I want to argue, however, that it goes further than that. I believe that it goes to the heart of what it means to lead. Pastors lead by providing God's people with the theological categories to make spiritual meaning.

> **Pastors lead by providing God's people with the theological categories to make spiritual meaning.**

The trajectory of scholarship supports this emphasis on leadership as meaning making. In the 1940s, scholars described personal traits that they thought made men (and it was men) accomplished leaders. These "trait theories" emphasized physical attributes (e.g., height and appearance), natural abilities (e.g., intelligence and eloquence), and personality characteristics (e.g., self-confidence). Over time, scholars recognized the bias of such studies and sought other explanations. For a few decades, then, scholars attributed success to an amorphous quality called "leadership style." They even proposed myriad schemata for segmenting the population according to the styles that they naturally practiced. Eventually scholars came to realize that these approaches left out an important component of leadership.[8]

In recent years, scholars have focused on the leader as a "manager of meaning." Such a leader, according to one insightful summary, "gives a sense of direction and of purpose through the articulation of a compelling worldview." It is "'sensemaking' on behalf of others [in order to] develop a social consensus around the resulting meanings." Such a perspective sees "leaders as managers of meaning rather than in terms of an influence process" and sees "the defining characteristics of leadership as the active promotion of values which provide shared meanings."[9] The view began with James McGregor Burns's notion of "transforming leadership"[10] and is summarized by Wilfred Drath and Charles Palus of the Center for Creative Leadership. "Leadership in organizations," they have said, is "more about making meaning than about making decisions and influencing people." In this context, "meaning-making is the process of creating names, interpretations, and commitments" to describe a situation. It "makes sense of an action by placing it in some larger frame."[11] This is exactly what Max DePree meant with his famous dictum, "The first responsibility of a leader is to define reality."[12]

Pastors sometimes have difficulty understanding what it means to "define reality." Let me illustrate this idea by looking at some of the phrases that Jesus used. In the Sermon on the Mount (see Matthew 5), for example, Jesus says, "You have heard that it was said . . . 'You shall not murder' . . . But I say to you . . . if you say, 'You fool,' you will be liable to the hell of fire" (vv. 21-22). "You have heard that it was said, 'You shall not commit adultery.' But I say to you that everyone who looks at a woman with lust has already committed adultery with her in his heart" (vv. 27-28). "It was also said, 'Whoever divorces his wife, let him give her a certificate of divorce.' But I say to you that anyone who divorces his wife, except on the grounds of unchastity, causes her to commit adultery, and whoever marries a divorced woman commits adultery" (vv. 31-32).

"Again, you have heard that it was said to those of ancient times, 'You shall not swear falsely, but carry out the vows you have made to the Lord.' But I say to you, Do not swear at all" (vv. 33-34). "You have heard that it was said, 'An eye for an eye, and a tooth for a tooth.' But I say to you, Do not resist an evildoer" (vv. 38-39). "You have heard that it was said, 'You shall love your neighbor and hate your enemy.' But I say to you, Love your enemies and pray for those who persecute you" (vv. 43-44).

In each case, Jesus is redefining reality. He is saying, in effect, "Once you understood adultery in this way, but from now on you shall understand it in a new way." He is trying to change the basic building blocks of people's perception: their ideas, their vocabulary, the theological categories they use. And by changing the definitions of the words, he is making new meaning. The penalty for murder still stands. So someone who demeans his neighbor is now liable as if he has committed murder. This is much more than simply changing a label. Giving a situation a new name implies that the response to that situation will change as well. When leaders like Jesus define reality, they set their people on a prescribed course

> This is how Christian leaders lead: they provide a theological framework for faithful action.

of action. And the reality that Christian leaders define is ultimately a spiritual reality. That is how they lead: they provide a theological framework for faithful action.

Charlotte Robinson provided such a framework when dealing with Gary Rivers. She told him that God had forgiven him and explained that the church was "in the forgiving business." Indeed, she was building on the work of some nameless pastor in Oklahoma who told Gary that he was a "new creation." The turning point for Gary was the point where he could say that "Old Man" Rivers was dead. The names that these pastors gave to explain circumstances allowed Gary to begin to walk the road to healing. Without these interpretative moments, Gary would still be trapped by feelings of guilt. By providing a definitive interpretation, the pastors were able to define Gary's reality. They shaped the very categories he used to judge himself and his relationship to the world around him.

The process of defining reality begins by understanding how people make meaning for themselves. The next section explains in detail how people come to interpret new situations. Once we understand this process, it becomes easier to see how to help people use theological categories to make spiritual meaning—and to understand a view of the leader as a theological interpreter rather than as someone who dictates policy.

A person makes meaning by focusing her or his attention on some things within a situation and by ignoring other things. The process begins, literally, with what a person sees—and what they fail to see. A person then arranges the things they see into a constellation. Ancient cultures across the world looked into the same heavens but they saw different things because they configured the stars by referencing their own unique stories. The Aztecs saw snakes and eagles; the Greeks saw Orion. In the same way, different people can see the same event and make very different sense of what they see. Charlotte Robinson saw Gary's return as a chance for healing; Laura Webber saw it as a threat to her reputation. They gave very different names to the same situation. Once a person such as you or me arranges events into a constellation, we of course give that constellation a name. We then think of the whole array as a single unit. This happens without our consciously knowing about it. But if a leader wants to take the next faithful step toward advanced Christian leadership, she or he will need to understand this sensemaking process. Specifically, leaders need to understand that:

1. Expectations filter what people see when they encounter a new situation.
2. Culture provides a repertoire of meanings for people to use in making sense of a particular situation.
3. Making sense involves composing stories out of culture's repertoire of meanings.
4. The interpretation we choose dictates the action we will take in response to the situation.
5. Those actions follow pre-legitimated paths.

Expectations Shape What We See

Sensemaking begins with what we see—and what we don't see. We learn early in life to filter what we see and hear, paying close attention to what's important and ignoring what is extraneous. There is simply too much information in the world to give full attention to everything. A dog barking in the distance is irrelevant, unless it's the familiar bark of your pet. Or, think about what happens when a teenager first sits behind the wheel of a car. When I was learning to drive, I paid too much attention to the cars parked on the side of the road and not enough attention to the Pontiac in front of me. I was sure one of those parked cars was going to leap out at me. But over time I learned that driverless cars were not going anywhere. If there was no one in the driver's seat, I could ignore a car. And if there were someone in there, I learned that my eye would be drawn to his or her movement and would single that car out for special attention. I also had to learn which street signs were important (e.g., No Left Turn, or Yield) and which signs could be ignored (e.g., Garage Sale, or Lost Dog). At first, everything got my attention. Then I learned to filter what I saw. That's when I was safe to drive on city streets.

The most rigorous driving lesson, however, takes place on the Los Angeles freeways, where the flow of traffic is often over eighty miles per hour. People come to California from Boston or New York and the freeways terrify them. In the East, it is not uncommon for someone to cross multiple lanes of traffic to make an unexpected lunge for the off-ramp. So transplanted Easterners expect it to happen on the Ventura Freeway. But that does not happen in Los Angeles. It's not so much that there are laws against such recklessness, although there are. It's more like Automotive Darwinism. If you drive erratically at eighty miles an hour, you die. So the Los Angeles freeways have become very predictable. But you have to know how to read the cues. That is, you have to know what information not to filter out. When a driver in front of you starts looking over her shoulder, you assume she's preparing to change lanes—whether or not she's used her turn indicator. And when you see three little leaguers bouncing in the back of a Volvo, you assume that the driver is distracted and give the car a wide berth. Learning to drive means learning to filter information—ignoring extraneous details but filing away the important ones. That's how we make sense of complicated situations.

But how do people decide what information to filter out, especially when they encounter new situations? The most powerful filter for information, it turns out, is also one of the subtlest. Expectations—especially unconscious expectations—shape what we see in our worlds. You would think that people wait to form their expectations until they have enough data for an interpretation. But it is just the opposite. People organize new data to fit their expectations. Think, for example, of first impressions. We form these impressions far more quickly than we realize. One Harvard study of teachers, for instance, tried to figure out how quickly people recognize good teaching. The researchers asked people to identify good teachers by watching videotapes of classrooms. They found that people judged the teachers very quickly. People who watched fifteen seconds of video reached the same conclusions as the people who watched for a half hour.[13] Then the researchers shortened the video clips. Eventually they discovered that people reached a consistent conclusion after viewing only two seconds of video. They arrived at their first impressions almost instantaneously. This is not to say that the first impressions were necessarily "correct" (good teaching is highly subjective). But the judgments people made in those first two seconds rarely changed. The impressions became self-fulfilling prophecies. This happens because, once we've formed impressions, we organize new data and new experiences according to what these impressions tell us to expect.

We unconsciously keep the data that fits our expectations and discard the data that does not. Studies of how people get jobs discuss this. If an interviewer gets a good first impression of a candidate, the interviewer will likely interpret the rest of what the candidate does in the best possible light. Say, for example, that a job candidate makes a joke halfway through the interview. Sometimes an interviewer will interpret that as indicating a "good sense of humor" (a positive trait), but other times the interviewer might write a note saying, "Everything's a joke to him. Not serious about work" (a negative trait). The joke provided new data that confirmed whatever impression the interviewer already had of the candidate. What the candidate said is neither inherently positive nor inherently negative; it is the expectation of the interviewer that determines the difference. Expectations are formed quickly and they become the key for organizing new experiences.[14]

The power of expectations is easily confirmed in daily life. One summer day, for example, I came back to my office at the school where I teach to find a phone message that said, "Kathy called." So I dialed the extension for Kathy Black, one of my colleagues. But her voice mail said that she was out of town. "Why would she be calling me from the road?" I wondered. So I phoned her secretary. No, the secretary said, she did not know anything about it. I began wondering if maybe the message was from another professor named Kathleen rather than Kathy. That did not make sense either. So I put the mystery aside for a bit and went about my business. I was stumped. Later that day I saw the person who took the message. She said that the caller said something about, "Melissa's birthday." And then I knew. Melissa is my niece. The caller was my sister.

Two things created expectations, which led me to a series of wrong conclusions, as I tried to make sense of the message. The first was context. I was at work. So the context made me expect that the call had something to do with my school. And, second, my sister spells her name "Cathy." I became confused from the very first letter of the note. When the message said "Kathy," I began searching my experience for women who spelled their names with a K. And even when I had exhausted the list of Kathys who related to my job, I did not go back and re-examine my assumptions. I did not look for "Cathys" nor did I look beyond my office context. Once I had formed the initial impression, I kept trying to find a way to get it to make sense. Even when there was new data that told me something was wrong; I did not go back. Expectations are so powerful that we contort our minds trying to find a way to confirm them. The expectations set us on a particular path. And once we are on that path, we are reluctant to leave it.

Let me illustrate further with another story from the Almond Springs congregation. In the first months of her tenure at Almond Springs, Rev. Charlotte Robinson met with the elders on the Worship Committee. She wanted their input as she planned her preaching for that first fall in town. As the conversation with the elders unfolded, it became clear that they were not going to offer strong opinions. One woman named Margo Gold seemed to be particularly difficult to move. Finally, she told the pastor to do what she was going to do. "But this is not my church," Charlotte said, "it belongs to all of its members." Margo would have none of it. Months later, Charlotte found out that Margo had been opposed to hiring a pastor because she believed that all pastors simply want to grab power. Indeed, she walked away from that initial Worship Committee meeting more distrustful of Charlotte than ever. The pastor tried to make her intention to share power clear by saying, "This is not my church." But Margo heard that as a ploy. It's as if Margo said to herself, "See, she's pretending to give us power. I knew she could not be trusted." Margo expected a pastor to grab for power. And she found a way to confirm that expectation, even if she had to distort Charlotte's meaning. A hearer's expectations are more powerful than a leader's intentions.[15]

> **A hearer's expectations are more powerful than a leader's intentions.**

Let me be clear, however, that Margo was not being malicious when she distorted Charlotte's meaning. We all find ways to confirm our assumptions. One reason we do this is that changing our assumptions can be painful. In fact, people often go through a grief process in giving up their assumptions. First they *deny* that what they expected to happen is not how things really are. *Blame* and *anger* often accompany the loss as well. I use the word "loss" because dashed expectations often leave a hole. Margo expected Charlotte to grab for power because that is how Margo understood all ministers. She saw them as men who asserted their authority. She did not see this view as idiosyncratic or controversial. In fact, she thought that it was a truism or a statement of fact—like saying that pastors preach sermons and visit the sick. It does us no good to ask where she came up with this notion because at this point in her life it is woven into her view of the world. And if someone were to try to change that view, it would feel like someone were tearing a hole in her world. I am not trying to be melodramatic here. But it is important to understand the pain we cause when we ask people to give up their expectations.[16]

Why spend so much space talking about expectations? Because growth requires people to give up their expectations. We will discuss this in detail later. But for now, think about the expectations people often have of ministers and how these expectations shape the way people judge a pastor. Every minister encounters these expectations. Some people believe that a pastor should visit the sick in the hospital. That means every sick person, including those

> Growth requires people to give up their expectations.

who are only marginally related to the congregation. And the expectations often extend to include something like clairvoyance—after all, the reasoning goes, the pastor should know when people are in the hospital. Almost every pastor has stories about how offended someone was because "no minister visited my father/mother/daughter/son/long-lost-cousin in the hospital." People don't think through the mechanics of how a pastor would know their father was in the hospital or that their mother required a pastoral visit. All they know is that "good pastors visit the sick and you didn't so you must not be a very good pastor." We are often judged by other people's expectations.

Other people's expectations are not the only part of this hospital misunderstanding. The pastor has expectations too. The pastor, for example, expected someone to call her about a needed visit. I was talking recently to a colleague about this moment of misunderstanding. She described her own years in pastoral ministry and the sadness (and anger) she often felt when she found out that a parishioner languished without her knowing it. She said that at some point in her ministry she had to realize that there was a certain absurdity to her expectations. Most people do not have experience with what happens when a loved one enters the hospital. In the midst of the fear and stress, they often do not think well. Every pastor knows that. And many people simply are not going to remember to call the pastor. They have too many other things on their minds. My friend realized that her expectation was unreasonable. So she tried to change her expectation. She tried to educate people who heard about a sick congregant to call the church, even if the person was not a family member. And she did something else as well. She shifted her understanding of blame. She no longer wanted to blame people for not calling her. She still had to accept the anger of people who blamed her for not visiting. (Other people's expectations that "the pastor should have known" remained unaffected by her insights.) But she knew that sometimes pastors have to bear people's anger even when the situation is not the minister's fault.

That is why visiting the sick turns out to be an easy example. A mature pastor well understands that she cannot feel responsible for unspoken needs (although the pastor will want to figure out how she could have found out about the needs). No, the harder situation comes when the pastor has to knowingly fail someone's expectations. For example, many parishioners believe things like: "pastors solve problems" or "if you love someone, you will shield them from pain." But there are plenty of moments when the most loving thing a leader can do is to let people solve their own painful problems. I can't tell a couple how to save their marriage. They have to do the hard and painful work of listening to each other's complaints and finding a way to make a life together. I am not with them when the husband has to decide whether or not to break his commitment to be home on time. And I can't be there when a wife gets a call from her husband saying that he has to fly one more time to Dallas on short notice. The hard decisions come from within—from within the person and from within the relationship. They have to do the work. And I have to fail that couple's expectations that I am the one who can make their marriage healthy again.

I may not be able to solve their problems, but I can help. I can listen, point them to resources, and ask them the hard questions that they would rather avoid. Ronald Heifetz has said that we have to fail people's "expectations at a rate they [can] stand."[17] What that means in this context is simply that pastors often have to fail the unrealistic expectations of parishioners (and of themselves). Many people expect, for example, that hiring a new pastor will make the congregation's problems disappear. Indeed many congregants greet the minister with two highly contradictive expectations. They expect the pastor to make the church grow and they expect the minister not to change anything. But growth is, by definition, change. People don't think through the implications of their conflicting expectations. In fact, they often do not know that they have such expectations. They only become aware of the expectations when someone does not measure up to them. So the pastor has to fail those expectations. But the new minister cannot simply announce on the first Sunday, "I am not the answer to your problems." The honeymoon would end right there. Nor can he say too quickly, "You are going to have to give up some things you cherish if you wish to grow." Again, people would not be ready for the message. A leader must fail people's expectations at a rate they can stand.

Expectations are tricky not just because people are often unaware of them. It goes further than that. The respected Harvard scholar Chris Argyris makes an important distinction between espoused theory and theory-in-use.[18] Espoused theory describes the reasons we give for our actions; theory-in-use describes the more complicated theory that explains how we actually behave. He's not talking about the times that we claim to be doing something for a noble reason but know in our heart of hearts that we have ulterior motives. That's only part of it. He is talking about the internal conversations where we explain our actions to ourselves—where we think we are doing one thing but we are really doing something a bit different. For example, I have worked hard to cultivate the practice of hospitality. I tell my students that they can drop by my office not just during office hours but whenever my light is on. I espouse this theory because I want to be the kind of professor who welcomes students. But there is a problem. Sometimes I am not in the mood to see people. Sometimes I have a pressing deadline. Or, as much as I hate to admit it, sometimes there are difficult students who I'd rather not have to deal with. So I sometimes listen politely and then send them on their way. I give them the appearance of hospitality without being particularly hospitable. I am not proud of this. And I try to stop myself when I realize I am doing it.[19] But the behavior illustrates Argyris's distinction. My espoused theory is hospitality. My theory-in-use is convenient hospitality (i.e., I will welcome people so long as it does not cost me too much). Every one of us espouses one thing while practicing another.

This distinction is germane to our discussion of self-fulfilling expectations because we often make sense of our own actions by filtering them through the lens of an espoused theory (or an espoused theology). I may look back on an encounter with a student and say to myself, "Of course I was not short with her. I value hospitality. I'm the guy who does not have office hours." My intent hides from me what actually happened. This is important both for what we do and what we observe. It should provide a loud caution for interpreting the moment when we disagree with someone else over what happened. I have to ask myself if my intentions are masking my true behavior.

The distinction also helps a leader understand other people. Sometimes I observe someone saying they are doing one thing while "obviously" doing another. For example, the Worship Committee was discussing the place of children in worship. At one point in the discussion, a congregant named Sue, known for her support of children, said, "Whole families should worship together because we are all part of the family of God and everyone should be accepted for who they are." But later in the conversation, she noted in passing that, "Of course, parents have a responsibility to keep kids quiet or take them out of the sanctuary." A fourth-grade teacher named Barry jumped on the comment. "Children are always noisy. That's who they are. You can't really say, Sue, that you value children if you just want them to be miniature adults."

There are at least three lessons to learn from this scene. First, Sue is not morally suspect for having a disparity between what she espoused and what she actually believed. She was not aware of the contrast and every one of us has such disparities. Second, Sue did not understand Barry's accusation. She must have been thinking, *"How can he say that about me? I started out by saying that children belong in worship."* In her mind, she was supporting children. And her espoused theology was the lens that she used to judge her own actions. And, third, there is a way for the leader to be proactive when someone may be espousing a theology that they may not be able to live out. Often the disparity either comes from unspoken caveats that the speaker has not anticipated or it derives from having competing commitments. In such situations, a leader can pose a hypothetical situation in order to get the speaker to name the qualifications they would put on their generalizations. So, in this case, the leader might ask Sue about what would happen if, say, a baby was crying during the sermon or a kid kept whispering to her mother during a prayer. Sue may well respond by saying that in such cases the parent should remove the child from the sanctuary. This would allow the leader to surface the competing commitments that separate the espoused theory from the theory-in-use by saying something like, "It sounds like you value two things and that some-times they conflict. You value the presence of children in worship because they are part of the family of God. And you believe each person should be able to worship without distractions. But the problem is that the two values, even positive values such as these, sometimes compete with each other. Kids will inevitably be distracting. So I think you are saying that you want the worship-without-distractions value to have priority over the children-are-part-of-God's-family value. I also think Barry would flip-flop those values. So I guess the next step for us is to have you, Sue, say if I've accurately described your values. And, if I have, then we should discuss together the priority of each."

This loops back to our discussion of expectations. People regularly have unspoken expectations about how their statements will be heard.[20] The expectations shape the way that a person understands the meaning of her own words. But others in the room often do not know about those expecta-tions. Indeed, the speaker her-self is often unaware of them. Sue did not realize that there were limits to her commitment

> Surface the competing commitments behind unspoken expectations.

to children in worship until that commitment bumped into other commitments.[21] Most people lack the self-awareness to know when they have created caveats to their espoused values. That means that one of the most important things a leader can do to help a group or person is to surface and to name the competing commitments behind unspoken expectations.

Charlotte Robinson felt this crosscurrent of expectations as she sat talking to Gary Rivers. Think of Gary's expectations about God and about church. He expected both God and the church to be judgmental in interpreting his repentance. Charlotte told him that God would forgive him and then she espoused a theology that said the church would too.

And, of course, we all believe that the church should be a place where people learn about God's forgiveness and find God's love. But even before Gary left the office, the pastor worried about the disparity between the theology that she espoused and the caveats that her congregation might well attach when practicing that theology. She said that he was forgiven, even as she knew there were congregants who were not ready to forgive him. This means that one of her first pastoral tasks in preparing the congregation to embody God's forgiveness to Gary will be for Charlotte to meet with Laura so that she can help Laura articulate and understand her own expectations about Gary. At some level, Laura expects Gary to bear her ex-husband's guilt because he could not stop Walt from beating Laura. Charlotte can tell that Laura's invective does not cohere with the person she knows Laura to be. But she also knows that it will take time for Laura to give up that expectation. And the pastor knows that giving up that blame will be painful. Laura has grown a lot as a person since she buried the pain that Gary's presence is bringing to the surface. Charlotte knows that it will take Laura some time to see that the theological view she now uses to interpret the world is inconsistent with that old blame. Whatever else Charlotte will have to do in this situation, a significant part of her pastoral work will be sitting with Laura as she manages the painful process of bringing her expectations in line with the theology that she espouses.

People will, in summary, construct meaning in a given situation based on the expectations they bring into the situation. This happens because expectations shape what people are able to see. A leader needs to be aware of the expectations that people bring to a situation, including the expectations that the pastor himself brings. The leader needs to recognize when someone's expectations are clouding the ability to make meaning. And the leader needs to help people through the painful process of aligning their expectations with their espoused theological commitments.

Culture Provides a Repertoire of Meanings

It is tempting, at this point, to think of meaning making as a rational process where observations lead to conclusions, which lead to action. But it turns out that people do not always follow an orderly or deductive formula when figuring out what a situation means. Instead, people engage in what Karl Weick calls "soliloquies." These are internal conversations that allow people to talk themselves into an interpretation of a given experience. The conversations play out in people's heads as they work to assign meaning in a new situation. This led Weick to conclude that, "soliloquies define cognition."[22]

> People talk themselves into an interpretation of a given experience.

The vocabulary of this internal conversation comes from the culture in which a person is embedded. A person might draw from popular culture (e.g., television cop shows), from ideas (e.g., when we talk about "rights"), from a trove of values (e.g., respect for elders), or, of course, from the Christian faith (e.g., love thy neighbor). We draw on a cache of cultural meanings that each of us carries with us in our minds.

This cache is part of what scholars call "culture."[23] We can "think of culture as the symbolic dimension of human activity and . . . its study, somewhat arbitrarily, as the study of discrete symbolic objects (art, literature, sermons, ideologies, advertisements, maps, street signs) and how they function in social life."[24] But there is a debate among scholars about whether or not culture constrains an individual's actions or whether it frees an individual to act.[25] On one hand, culture can restrict the options available to a person. For example, there are only two primary positions on abortion in America. And, no matter what a pastor or a politician says to nuance her position, the public will eventually put her in the pro-choice camp or align her with the pro-life contingent. The culture does not provide room for a middle ground. Some scholars see this as a paradigm for how culture constrains our ability to act. We can, according to this view, only choose between the options that the society says are legitimate choices. On the other hand, we have tremendous freedom in how we use those choices. According to the alternate view, culture is a tool kit that allows us to construct whatever actions we desire by using the diverse array of tools that the culture provides—tools like ideas, values, stories, and identities.[26] I think it is important to acknowledge the wisdom in each of these views of culture. It is true that there are only a limited number of choices available to me as I decide how to act in a certain situation—and that I can only choose from symbols that have "legitimacy" (we'll say more about that soon). But it is just as true that I can mix and match the symbols that culture provides in creative ways that allow me a tremendous range of options. In short, a person can only choose from cultural symbols that have been "legitimated," but that person can then rearrange those symbols to engage in almost any action.

A quick example of this freedom and this constraint involves Rev. Charlotte Robinson's range of options in response to Gary Rivers's confession. Charlotte could respond as a woman with outrage that Gary would strike his wife and that he would leave Laura vulnerable to Walt's repeated abuse. She could respond as Laura's friend and seek to hide Gary from public display because she knows it will embarrass her friend. Instead, Rev. Robinson chose to respond as Gary's pastor proclaiming a message of forgiveness and hope.[27] The culture provided a repertoire of options from which Charlotte could draw in constructing a meaningful response to Gary's confession.

The word *repertoire* is particularly evocative because it weds a way of seeing the world with a way of performing in it. The concept comes from the sociologist Ann Swidler, who has said that, "perhaps we do best to think of culture as a repertoire, like that of an actor, a musician, or a dancer." We can see in the church that people develop different repertoires. Some people cultivate a facility, say, with the Bible. They can quote many verses and know all about its history. Other people, say, have nurturing personalities that allow them to express deep sympathy. And, perhaps a third group of people loves to play games, learning to strategize into the future while enjoying the thrill of the moment. The repertoire "image suggests that culture cultivates skills and habits in its users." A person can be "good at the cultural repertoire one performs." This means that "such cultured capacities may exist both as discrete skills, habits, and orientations and, in larger assemblages, like the pieces a musician has mastered or the plays an actor has performed."[28] We can each draw on a range of repertoires in interpreting the world.

Each of us learns many repertoires, even from a young age. And they shape how we see the world. For example, one of the repertoires that formed my particular personality came from playing team sports as a child. I learned early on the importance of sacrificing one's individual goals for the sake of a communal goal. I learned how to trust other people and how to be trustworthy so that my teammates could rely on me. And, because it is as much fun to throw the pass as it is to make the basket, I learned to get satisfaction from helping someone else excel. These are all positive traits that I like very much about myself. But there are also negative lessons that came with the team sports repertoire, lessons I have worked hard to unlearn. I used to see the world as a competition; I saw other people as players who could be used to accomplish my ends; and, I often wanted a referee to step in when I thought I had been treated unfairly. I recognize these tendencies for what they are and try to curb them—even though astute readers will no doubt find vestiges of those instincts latent in this text. But that's the way cultural repertoires come to us, as prepackaged collections of "skills, habits, and orientations." The sacrifice-self-for-the-good-of-the-team part of the sports repertoire comes bound up with the life-as-competition part of the repertoire. That is why Swidler calls them prepackaged collections.[29]

People then use the repertoires or the tools that are most familiar to them. We've all heard the adage that "when all you have is a hammer, everything looks like a nail." So when I was a young adult, I saw the world as a competition and used my team-sports mentality to engage the world. I did not see myself as selecting one from many options of how to understand the world. I assumed that all people in all places must see the world the way I did—because I assumed that I was seeing the world as it really existed. But over time I became aware of a problem. As I child, I also learned the repertoire of the Christian faith. And I began to see that the values of the Christian faith (say, gentleness, hospitality, and kindness) were often at odds with the values that came as part of my life-as-team-sport worldview.

So I found that faithfulness to God required me to learn a new repertoire. This was slow—often-painful—work. One year, for example, the focus of my spiritual disciplines could be summarized in two words: "cultivate gentleness." I studied gentleness in Scripture, I planned out ways to practice it in daily life, and I prayed that God would make gentleness manifest in my life. Indeed, gentleness became the name I gave to a whole repertoire of behaviors (like empathetic listening) and attitudes (like patience).[30] Oftentimes I felt like an awkward teenager learning to waltz. The steps did not always come naturally to me. My sports instincts clashed with the Christian instincts I was cultivating. But I persevered because I value gentleness and I knew it was not a part of my repertoire. I now find, after many years, that I can practice gentleness quite comfortably—but that it slips away in times of stress or when I don't get enough sleep. Like any other art, I find that the more I learn about gentleness the farther I have to go in practicing it. But I am trying to cultivate it as a part of my repertoire.

Understanding the clash between repertoires is particularly important for the meaning-making leader. Every leader will encounter moments when they will have to cultivate new repertoires for themselves. They will also be in a position when they will have to help others expand their repertoires. This is necessary because the clash of repertoires often points to blind spots and gaps in faithfulness. Defensive reasoning[31] is the by-product of an inability to recognize when it is time to cultivate a new repertoire. In this way, a leader has to remember the old adage that "our greatest strengths contain our greatest weaknesses." The very repertoires where we are most proficient often contain within them the blind spots that handicap a leader. For example, I know a leader who exudes confidence, even in the face of criticism. As a former pastor and a former politician, he could draw on more than one repertoire in leading his religious organization. And he was able to carry that organization, which was teetering on the brink of collapse, into a new life of renewed stability. Part of the reason he succeeded in that moment was that he drew from his politician's repertoire an ability to ignore the naysayers who called for caution. Instead, he forged a bold new path. His confident ability to discount those who disagreed was one of his greatest strengths. But the same confidence in his own abilities represented one of his greatest weaknesses. He regularly clashed with other staff members in the organization who had a legitimate expectation for input into the organization's future direction. His politician's repertoire allowed him to make promises that he could not really expect to fulfill.[32] He saw people pleasing as the cost of doing business. This politician's confidence, however, clashed with his organization's expectations about how a pastor should act. Indeed, the organization eventually outgrew him because he was never able to blend the repertoires of pastor and politician. Our greatest strengths often contain our greatest weaknesses.

A repertoire contains more than attitudes and behaviors. It also holds ideas, stories, experiences, and feelings. For example, the organizational structure of one of the largest American denominations took on its particular form because a few people had within their repertoire a paradigmatic experience, one that they did not want to repeat. And when it came to understanding organizations, that experience was the most salient part of their repertoire. When the denomination was reorganizing its mission structures, the denomination convened meetings throughout the country, commissioned surveys, and engaged scholars to determine the most theologically appropriate and organizationally effective way to do mission. They came up with a preliminary plan. But at a crucial moment in the debate, a few key leaders said that the proposed structure reminded them of an organization in which they had once worked. Those key leaders were determined that the new structure would not repeat the mistakes of their past. So the leaders quietly reconfigured the plan, turning it inside out and nullifying the year of study that prepared the proposed plan. In other words, the paradigmatic experience of a few key people was more powerful than the combined wisdom of the rest of the denomination. Now, let me be clear. I am not saying that those leaders were incorrect in their assessment or that the structure they proposed was better or worse than the one that they jettisoned. What I am saying, however, is that we, as leaders, have to be careful about how we weigh evidence and make sense of new experiences. Those leaders judged that the proposed structure was deficient because it did not measure up to the standards of their experiences. These leaders espoused an ethic of consultation that said that the new structure would reflect the wisdom of the whole denomination. But when it came time to make a meaningful decision, their theory-in-use said that they would accept the wisdom of the whole people so long as it did not contradict the wisdom of their collective experience. The most salient meaning in their cultural repertoire was their collective experience.

People Interpret New Situations by Weaving Stories from Culture's Repertoire of Meanings

The tools a person chooses to use will determine the meanings available to them. Think, for instance, about what it means to be a Christian. Some people emphasize theology and define Christianity as set of beliefs. Others see it as a moral stance and define it by its values. There are hosts of other ways to define Christianity. And each one draws on a different cultural tool or plays on a different part of the cultural repertoire. We will describe these tools in greater detail when we talk in part 2 about the specific work of a leader. But for now the important point is that how you make sense of important questions depends on which part of the cultural repertoire you find most comfortable.

Consider, for example, the often-debated question as to whether America is a Christian nation. Those who emphasize a theological definition might say that the nation is not "Christian" because the majority of Americans do not hold to the beliefs that that group would say are the essence of the faith. Other people might argue, by emphasizing a different cultural resource (e.g., values or history), that America is indeed a Christian nation. You, no doubt, have your own opinion. Stop reading for a moment and state aloud your view. Do you believe America is a Christian nation? Pay attention to the rationale you give for your answer to the question. Perhaps you want to jot down your reasons. The result you come up with will depend on which cultural resources you choose to muster.

> Do you believe America is a Christian nation?

The internal debate you may have just had over the question of a Christian America deserves a bit more attention. You are likely reading this on your own. You are not presently in a group of people debating the question. And that distinction is also an important part of how you make meaning. Look back at what you wrote down. Are there parts of your answer that you feel more strongly about than others? So long as the question is purely hypothetical (i.e., so long as nothing is at stake) then it is relatively easy to answer the question.

Now picture yourself in a more controversial setting. Perhaps a parishioner has vehemently articulated the position that is exactly opposed to your own. And suppose that this ardent parishioner is questioning you about your answer to the question. Your answer to the very same question, according to Swidler's research, would likely be different under those circumstances. She found that people who were actively defending a position or stance use cultural resources differently from those people who are simply trying to make sense of a situation.[33] In the heat of a controversy, a person will use any tool they can grab in order to buttress their point. Someone being challenged likely will not worry about making sure their argument is internally consistent or if there are countervailing points. They will heap one cultural resource atop another like a homeowner piling sandbags in the face of a flood.

The other thing that happens, especially under stress, is that people sift through the resources available to them and modify those cultural resources to their own ends. For example, Swidler tells the story of a middle-class couple experiencing marital difficulties. They consulted both a minister and a therapist. The couple used some of what they heard, but discarded the rest. They chose to ignore, for instance, one piece of advice that they heard from both of the experts.[34] The therapist and the minister each told the couple that the husband had to do what was best for himself and the wife had to do what was best for herself. The experts said that if the couple's interests coincided the marriage would continue and if they diverged the marriage would end. The couple ignored this advice, however, because their first priority was to save the marriage. They both wanted to stay married. So they filtered out any advice that they thought might lead them on separate paths. Some of what the experts advised proved helpful. But they appropriated only those resources that would help them accomplish their goal. Swidler sees their actions as paradigmatic. "When people appropriate cultural materials," she found that people appropriate "only what they could use and [leave] the rest . . . adapt[ing] them to their own purposes."[35]

Swidler found that people make sense of their worlds differently when they are not under pressure. Weick may have described cognition as a soliloquy, but Swidler sees it as storytelling. People look for the story that makes the most sense of a situation. "Cultural frameworks," she has said, "tend to be organized around imagined situations . . . Indeed a cultural repertoire remains diverse partly because it contains frameworks for making sense of many different scenes or situations."[36] For example, my church is large enough that I sometimes see a child crying in the social hour after worship. Met with a crying child, I have to figure out what the situation means. Usually I observe the parent's face to get a clue. I can often distinguish an angry parent from a concerned parent. And, when I see an angry parent, I often read the situation as, "The child has done something wrong and is now crying because she is in trouble." And, when I see a concerned parent, I look for further cues like a scraped knee. Then I might conclude that the child fell down and has injured herself. But notice how much the very language I use to explain the sensemaking presumes a story. In the first instance, I did not say simply that the child misbehaved. I drew it out so that it composed a scene. The child got caught and is now crying because she is in trouble. It falls naturally into a scene from a larger story. Likewise, when I describe a child scraping a knee, I hearken back to all the times when I scraped my knee as a child and all the times I hugged my daughters when they scraped their knees. The story has a background

> People look for the story that makes the most sense of a situation.

and it has connotations (e.g., scraped knees are not serious injuries). The most natural way for me to make sense of a new situation is to put it into a story.

This story-shaped logic applies even when people are engaged in what would appear to be abstract thinking. Swidler interviewed people about the concept of love. And she found that they did not display the deductive process that one usually associates with rational thinking. We tend to think that, at their best, people use abstract ideas like beliefs and values to come to some pristine conclusion and that they then apply that abstract conclusion to the specific situation at hand. Swidler found that such is not the case. "People are little constrained by logic," she found. And that's why "logical deduction rarely influences social action directly."[37] Instead, people told stories. There were key narratives that repeated themselves in her interviews. In some cases, people defined themselves over against the paradigmatic stories. For instance, many people claimed not to subscribe to the "Hollywood ideal" of marriage, which seemed to be that a couple falls madly in love, overcomes some obstacle, and then lives happily ever after. The respondents used this image to say that love was hard work. But they did not offer a principle or a generalization. Instead, they told the story of the Hollywood ideal and then added that love was not like that. There were also paradigmatic examples that served as positive ideals.

But Swidler found something more important. Stories were not just illustrations. People constructed their ideas about love by playing out stereotypic scenes in their heads. People talked, for example, about balancing individual needs against the needs of the other person. Swidler concluded that, "Their cultural understandings of love are organized not around the logical coherence of a single image, metaphor, or theory of love but around a core situation or problem."[38] That is, as people worked out strategies for dealing with similar situations, they came to similar generalizations about love.

To come up with these generalizations, they often played out competing scenarios in their minds and selected the story whose ending matched their own ideals. Let me illustrate how this works by describing what happened when the Almond Springs Presbyterian Church interviewed for their choir director opening.

"I'll bet you money that he's gay,"[39] Margo Gold mumbled to Joe Bellini as they waited for the joint meeting of the Worship Committee and Personnel Committee to start. Joe was puzzled. He looked down at the resumes for the candidates: Herb Wallstark and Darien Hill.

"What are you talking about?" Joe asked, a bit incredulous.

"Look at what we know about Darien," she said. "He's a clean-cut, thirty-two-year-old musician who lives with his mother. You know he's got to be gay." Before Joe could respond, the Rev. Charlotte Robinson called everyone to order and began the meeting.

The first candidate was Herb Wallstark. He had been a choir director in Maryland, serving in various Methodist and Presbyterian churches. He and his new wife had just moved to California to be near her daughter, who lived in Fresno. "I've worked in a number of small churches," he said, "so I know how it works. The key is finding interesting music so that people will want to be part of the choir." The pastor asked him a theological question about baptism. He explained how the question required a different response in a Presbyterian church than it did in a Methodist congregation, a distinction that was lost on most of the laypeople in the room. After he left, almost everyone in the room seemed to think he was an acceptable but unexciting candidate. The only exception was Margo, who spoke at length about Herb's virtues.

Then the committees met with Darien Hill. He was a computer programmer in Fresno, a job that he thought he might keep even if he were hired as the choir director. He had sung in a number of choirs and even founded a choral group in college. "I've been shaped by two encounters with death," he said earnestly in response to a question about his beliefs. "When I was twenty-six years old, my fiancé, Cassandra, rolled her car on the old highway not too far from here. She slipped in and out of a coma for a few weeks, and then she was gone." His voice was clear, but there was still pain in the memory. "Not long after that, they discovered my mother had breast cancer. After a year or so, I moved in with her to take care of her the best I could. I had to put aside my music. There just was not time. She passed away three months ago." He stopped to take a breath. "I want this job so that I can rediscover music. I've put off God's call to me while I was with Mom. But now I'm ready to return to my love." As he finished his story, a few people dabbed their eyes. The only substantive question that came in the ensuing conversation was from the pastor. She asked him the same "sacrament of baptism" question she'd asked Herb. Darien smiled gently at the question, "I am not sure what a sacrament is," he began with a self-deprecating chuckle, "but I can tell you that baptism is a time of joy because a lost lamb has returned to God's fold." The committees smiled too; they liked him.

The committee's conversation about the candidates illustrates how people use stories to make sense of new situations. On paper, Herb was far more qualified than Darien. But as the committee talked with Darien they found out that the reason he did not have as much experience was that he had been caring for his elderly mother. This was the first job that he had pursued since she died. There were some on the committee who wanted to give Darien a break. "I feel for the guy," Joe Bellini said, "It's not his fault that he does not have as much experience. We should not penalize him for doing the right thing and caring for his mother." Margo did not agree, "But Herb has a lot more experience. Even if Darien had spent the last decade as a choir director, he could not have accumulated enough experience to match Herb." The conversation went back and forth in this way for a few frustrating minutes. After awhile, the committee asked Rev. Robinson what she thought. She talked about the difficulty that they had endured with the previous choir director and about how she hoped that the next choir director could be part of a team. Then she concluded, "It's not Darien's lack of experience that is the problem as much as the fact that he does not understand theology very well. When we asked him about the sacrament of baptism, he admitted that he did not even know what the term meant. I am afraid he has too much ground to make up." In the end, the congregation selected Herb. But the reason it took so long was the sympathy that the committee felt for Darien.[40]

There are a number of lessons to learn about sensemaking from this story. First, people mix and match stories. They adopt a framework for interpreting a situation and play out the story that that framework suggests. But if they get to a dead end or come to a problem that their narrative framework cannot resolve, people then jump to a new frame. They neither start all over again, nor are they troubled if the second framework is inconsistent with the first framework. The logic of the two strategies does not need to have any clear connection because people string together different frameworks to make sense of situations. This is what Margo did. She initially opposed Darien because she thought he was gay. So, as she listened to Herb, she composed a story that put him in the best possible light. She saw him as an experienced and dedicated professional because she was predisposed not to support Darien. And even when she discovered that her initial assumption about Darien was incorrect, it did not change the story that she had composed to evaluate Herb. She had gone too far down the path to turn back and examine the false assumptions that had got her there. Just as I could not reexamine my expectations when I thought Kathy (rather than Cathy) had left me a message, so Margo was unaware of the degree to which she was already invested in her story for making sense of Darien and Herb. So she changed the telling of the story, but not its ending. At first, she said to herself, "Darien is gay, so Herb is better." But when she discovered that Darien was not gay, she said instead, "Darien is inexperienced, so Herb is better." She was so invested in her story that she had to find a way to change its telling without changing its conclusion.

Second, people compare competing stories in order to see which one makes the most sense of a situation. For example, Margo would normally have been worried by Herb's recent marriage and his multiple divorces. Under different circumstances, Herb could have reminded her of her ex-husband. But Margo chose not to explore that scenario because she did not want to have to oppose Herb. In judging which story makes the most sense, people often compare the end of the story to a pre-legitimated standard. That's exactly what Margo did. She believed that being gay was worse than being a bad husband. So she decided that Herb had to be better than Darien. Without knowing it, she compared the outcomes of the two ways of making sense of the candidates and chose the story with the conclusion she wanted to achieve.[41]

Third, people reason according to what scholars call "sympathetic identification." That is, they feel a connection to a character in a story and thus see the situation through that character's eyes. The characters do not have to be people either. Ansel Richards, the environmentalist in Almond Springs, identified with the plants and animals of nature. If he had said, "How would you feel if someone uprooted your home?" that would be sympathetic identification. When a person identifies with a character in a story, that person is likely to judge the story with a bias toward the interests of the sympathetic character.

Rational theologizing and sympathetic identification are sometimes in tension with one another. The committee interviewing Darien (with the exception of Margo) felt a sympathetic connection with him. They liked him and wanted to find a way to hire him as much as Margo wanted to find a reason not to hire him. Joe Bellini wanted to find a way to excuse Darien's lack of experience because Darien had been caring for his sick mother. But we can easily imagine a scenario where Darien could have rubbed Joe the wrong way—say, by the way he dressed or the attitude he adopted. In such a case, we can imagine Joe not being so charitable toward Darien. The sympathy Joe felt led him to give Darien a break. But the committee eventually reached an impasse when Joe's sympathy clashed with Margo's antipathy toward Darien. That's when they turned to the pastor, who applied a direct logic. And that logic (and the credibility of the pastor to make that judgment) tipped the scale in Herb's favor.

The Darien example emphasizes the sympathy part of sympathetic identification, but there are also times when people reason by identifying with someone—that is, they put themselves in the other person's place. And they then interpret the situation to the advantage of the person with whom they identify. Such reasoning can be a problem because a person (say, a middle-aged, white dad) will naturally gravitate toward the perspective of people who are similar (and not toward, say, a Hispanic teen). And, to make matters worse, a person tends to objectify a person who is dissimilar. Combine the sympathetic pull in with the objectifying push away and it becomes clear, for example, why juries need to be diverse: to combat the natural tendency of a white dad not to believe a Hispanic teen because the older man cannot identify with the younger man.

Reasoning by sympathetic identification is not, however, always a problem. Sometimes sympathetic identification can also work as a bridge to theologizing. The innovative religious educator Mary Hess uses media (especially television and movies) to break down the walls that teens often erect to fend off new ideas.[42] She shows movies that ease the youth into situations where they are on the other side of a question. And when they begin to identify with the protagonist in a story, she asks the teens theological questions to get them to understand people who are not like themselves. Religious leaders sometimes use a similar method when working with adults. Again, the goal is to personalize an issue, which is the opposite of objectifying. For example, opponents of the death penalty use the movie, *Dead Man Walking*, to help people see a condemned prisoner as a human being rather than as a "criminal" without a face. Proponents of the death penalty, likewise, tell stories of the suffering the inmate caused. In each case, the advocates want the public to identify with a person—either the person on death row or the grieving family of the victim. Leaders personalize issues by creating stories that allow people to feel a sympathetic identification with someone else's plight.

What leadership lessons can we draw from how Charlotte acted in this search for a choir director? She was not much of a role model. She was relatively passive. The congregation missed a lot of data in its debate about the two candidates. And she fixated on one distinction—the ability to explain theology—and used that to define the candidates.

A more helpful approach from the leader would have been for her to do a bit of orientation with the committees before the candidates arrived. She could explain that our first impressions often deceive us. And she could say that each person was going to have to work hard to listen both for things that confirm and for things that disconfirm their expectations. Then she could ask people to name their expectations in advance. She could then ask them to write down data in the interview that supports their expectations and for data that does not support their expectations. This would cultivate an expectation that it would be appropriate to change one's mind. She could also name her own expectations up-front. For example, she could evaluate what the difficult relationship with the previous choir director taught her, namely that she values a choir director who will work as part of a staff team. She could also say that theological training is important to her. Finally, she could manage the discussion after the interviews by asking people to share what they wrote down—emphasizing how their impressions might have changed. In so doing, she might well have ended up hiring Darien instead of Herb.[43]

People compose stories to make meaning in a situation. For example, Margo composed a story that said Darien was gay and concluded from it that the other candidate would be a better choir director. The stories often compete with one another because there is more than one way to make sense of a situation. Joe Bellini, on the other hand, composed a story that said that Darien was inexperienced because he had cared for his ailing mother. Joe's story for making sense of Darien thus was in competition with Margo's story. This leaves

> People use the repertoires of culture to construct stories that make meaning.

people a number of options. In this case, the competing stories essentially cancelled each other out, leaving Charlotte's statement about their theological abilities as the key observation. Under conditions of stress, people will select the stories that offer them the greatest advantage. When people are not feeling attacked, they might look at the end result of competing stories and select the one that appeals to them. Or, they might feel the sway of sympathetic identification and interpret the situation from a particular character's perspective. People use the repertoires of culture to construct stories that make meaning.

The Interpretation Dictates the Action

Meaning making is inherently active. Leaders need to recognize that when people make meaning—or when a pastor channels a group toward a particular interpretation—the meaning that they assign to a situation sets them on a course of action. In other words, there is a tight relationship between the interpretation of a situation and the action taken in response to that situation. When I saw the police arresting the "suspects" in the white sedan, I exhaled in relief without thinking about it. The interpretation led immediately to the action. This happens often when people make sense of a situation. Let me illustrate this point with the following example. I will describe a situation and then ask you to interpret it.

Mindy is a sixteen-year-old who attends a Lutheran church in a midwestern suburb called Woodside. She has remained a faithful member of the congregation even though her parents stopped coming after they divorced eighteen months ago. Mindy is a regular part of the congregation's four-person youth choir, attends the denomination's regional youth rallies, and is the only teen to participate in the congregation's intergenerational nursing home visitation program. She is a gifted student who almost always has a book in tow. In the last few months, she's put aside romance novels to take on more spiritual fare. She began by reading C. S. Lewis and recently waded through a substantial biography of Martin Luther. While investigating Luther for a term paper in World History, she found on the Internet what she calls "women's liturgies" that replace masculine references to God with gender inclusive terms. Driving back from the nursing home one Sunday, she ended up in the front seat of a mini-van sitting next to the pastor. In the back seat, a knot of senior citizens was kibitzing about the Cardinals and the Cubs. As they drove across town, the pastor tried as casually as possible to ask Mindy if she prayed every day. "Sure," she said, "I kinda do what Luther did. I baptize myself each morning." "Oh, really," the intrigued pastor said. "Yeah," she continued, "I wrote my own little prayer. And basically each morning I kinda put my hand on my head and, you know, say, 'You are a child of God. God's your mother. God's your father. God will never leave you.'"

> **What do you make of Mindy's daily ritual?**

Before I continue the story, I would ask you to think about what you've heard so far. Ask yourself how you would make sense of this situation. What are the key elements of the scene? What do you make of Mindy's daily ritual? Put yourself in the pastor's place, driving the van in the seat next to her. What would you say to her? Think for a moment before you move on to the next paragraph. Perhaps you want to write down your thoughts.

People respond to the story in any number of ways. I'll describe some of those responses. You may have written down any or all of them. Or you may have come up with ones I do not list here. The point is not to look for a right answer but instead to show that no matter which interpretation you chose that there is an action associated with it. Some people who respond to the situation are heartened that a teenage girl takes her faith seriously, thrilled that someone so young has the maturity (or innocence) to become her own priest. Some people identify with the girl and want to encourage her in any way they can (this is a common reaction of people who work with youth). Other people who hear the story worry about particular theological issues such as the female imagery for God or that a nonordained person is "baptizing." Still other people immediately psychologize the situation by connecting the parental content of Mindy's prayer to her parents' recent divorce. Very few people point to all of the above at once. They focus in on a few details and make those details the backbone of the story they tell themselves to interpret her actions. For those who tell a teen-faith story, the most important details are Mindy's age and her earnestness in expressing her faith. For those who theologize her answer, the key details are the ways that her prayer diverges from established beliefs. And those who psychologize emphasize the pain divorce causes for children and the tendency people have to project parental issues onto God. The meaning a person assigns to the scene depends on which details they use to make it part of a larger story.

Let me emphasize that very few people put all these details together into their story. It would not necessarily be helpful if they did. There are too many divergent details to come up with a simple story. And all the situation requires for action is a simple narrative logic. The important point here is not which story you created when you interpreted the story for yourself. The important point is that you created a story and the way that the story then leads naturally to action.

I say that a story leads naturally to action because, once a person decides what the story means, it is a very short step to deciding what one should do in response to the situation. Those who cheer at Mindy's theological chutzpah want to encourage her. Those who fret about theological error want to gently correct her. And those who psychologize the story want to probe her emotions to see if the ritual is a warning sign. The action you and I take in response to a situation is inextricably tied to the meaning we assign to it.

In fact, people often have difficulty separating the meaning they assign from the action they take. For example, when some conservatives discuss the case, they are reluctant to assign too much importance to the feminine language that in other contexts would alarm them. The reason for this is that they have well-defined scripts for what to do when someone is in theological error. Error should be corrected, they believe. But these reluctant conservatives often feel sympathetic identification with Mindy as well. They do not want to have to be too hard on her. They want to encourage her, so they downplay the importance of the theological content. In other words, they play the scenario out in their heads. And they choose the encourage-her-attempts-at-faith outcome rather than the correct-her-error outcome. They know that a strict judgment on theology will necessitate an equally strict response to the earnest young girl. And, because they don't like the results of the strict theological interpretation, they find a different way to make sense of the story.

The scene thus illustrates two important points. First, it shows how people play out competing narratives for making sense of a situation, allowing them to select the interpretation that makes the story come out the way that they think it should. And, second, it shows the tight connection between action and interpretation.

We can see how this idea connects to making spiritual meaning by returning to the Old Man Rivers episode from Almond Springs. First of all, we can see that specifically spiritual meaning making in this case involves using theological categories and plotlines to make sense. When the pastor takes up the biblical theme of the "new creation," it helps Gary understand his life using a specifically spiritual plotline. It says to Gary that God has acted in his life to transform him and that the result of God's action is that Gary himself is a new being. Charlotte Robinson could extend that story with him by showing how his being a new creation sets him on a new path of action. She could point to the full reference that says, "If anyone is in Christ, that one is a new creation. Behold, the old has passed away and the new has come" (2 Cor. 5:17). She could use the verse to remind Gary that he no longer has to live in fear about forgiveness.

In other words, the interpretation (i.e., that Gary is a new creation) is tied to action (i.e., that Gary can put away his fears because God has promised not to hold his sin against him). But there is also the question of how the whole congregation is to make spiritual sense of Gary's longing for forgiveness. Charlotte wants to help them see that if God has forgiven Gary, then they should too. One way to do that would be to rely again on the 2 Corinthians passage that Gary himself referenced. It goes on to say that God has given to all Christians a "ministry of reconciliation." By introducing this language of reconciliation, Charlotte might address many of the concerns that need to be interpreted. The language implies an estrangement, which is certainly present. And it allows Gary a forum for taking responsibility for his complicity in the destructive abuse. He can publicly acknowledge that his actions were sinful and he can make the public confession that will be crucial to his healing. But it also implies the action that the community of faith should take if it wants to act faithfully in response to Gary's repentance. By providing a theological framework (in this case from 2 Cor. 5), the pastor can cast the situation in an interpretative light and set both Gary and the congregation on the path to faithful action.

There is a problem, however, with the means of addressing the problem—as you have no doubt already seen. It does not address Laura's concerns. As Charlotte says, her friend is not going to want to be seen as a victim. And a public confession from Gary is (as it presently stands) going to dredge up some unpleasant feelings for Laura. Indeed, the phone call that opens the episode suggests that it already has. Thus, the pastor has a prior meaning-making task, one that she needs to perform before she can put Gary in front of the congregation. She is going to have to help Laura construct an alternate framework for interpreting Gary's return. Right now, it means little more than the opening of old wounds. Charlotte needs to sit with Laura and listen long enough to win the right to help Laura create a new interpretation. Perhaps the pastor can help her parishioner see the damage that comes from unresolved pain. Laura may well be strong enough now to revisit the things that were once too painful to fully examine. We don't know for sure what Charlotte could do because we don't know enough about Laura's circumstances (that is why Charlotte has to listen). But we do know what the pastor's strategy should be. She should listen long enough that she could help Laura construct a more faithful interpretation for the meaning of Gary's return.

There is one more way that the Old Man Rivers episode illustrates the points we have been discussing. The actions that Charlotte decided to take flowed as the natural by-product of the interpretations she assigned to the events. She believed that Gary Rivers had been forgiven by God. She did not decide to forgive him. That was not her place. But she interpreted Gary's actions using Psalm 51, which says that God would honor a "broken and contrite heart." Once she assigned this meaning to the situation, she had no choice in her pastoral role but to follow God's lead and proclaim assurance of pardon to her contrite parishioner. In like manner, Charlotte decides that Laura is broken in a way that we are all broken. She then makes sense of Laura's situation by seeing it through the lens of human brokenness. In each case, the action flows directly from the interpretation. And the tricky part for the leader is to find a way for the two interpretations (and actions) to cohere.

Actions Follow Pre-legitimated Paths

Such a tight connection between action and interpretation exists because we follow pre-legitimated avenues to action. Legitimacy is a crucial concept for leaders to understand. Legitimacy is the closest thing to a bottom line that exists for meaning making. When we make sense of a situation, how do we decide if our interpretation is a good one? Or if we hear someone else make an interpretation, how will we determine if it is appropriate? We cannot compare meaning to some external standard. Nor can we decide if Interpretation A makes three units more sense than Interpretation B. We have to make subjective judgments. That's why people often do little more than select the action they want to take and then find an interpretation that allows them to justify it. But it would be too cynical to assume that all situations come down to little more than self-interested rationalizing. Some interpretations make more sense to us than others. The ones that make the most sense are usually the ones with the most legitimacy.

Legitimacy is the phrase that organizational scholars use to describe the mechanism that decides when something "is defined by a set of social norms as correct or appropriate."[44] The important part of the definition is the fact that "social norms," or what we have called culture, determine what is correct or appropriate. For example, think of neckties. When I preach or when I teach, I wear a necktie as a symbol of the office that I occupy—either as a pastor or a professor. It is not uncommon, when I preach, for silver-haired women to complement me on how I look. What they are saying, in effect, is, "You look the way that we want a pastor to look." When I first started in ministry, I was especially careful to "dress appropriately" because my young age sometimes made people nervous. The necktie reassured them. But there are congregations where just the opposite would be the case. Their preachers wear baggy Hawaiian shirts and leather sandals in order to signal that preachers can relate to the lives their congregants lead. In such a place, my necktie would be off-putting, a symbol that I was out of touch. It would, in other words, be inappropriate. The symbol that marks legitimacy in one context can be de-legitimating in another arena.

Let me give another example of how legitimacy works, one that focuses on the one thing that you and I share—an experience of this book. When I was writing this book, I talked with groups of pastors about how to improve it. One common theme that often arises when ministers discuss my work is the question of appropriate sources. No one questions that it is legitimate for me to quote Jesus or to tell stories about congregations. But some folks feel uncomfortable when the book quotes secular sources like sociological studies. The business-oriented literature is particularly controversial. I have a set of criteria that I use in determining which sources can help us understand congregations and which ones violate the logics of the faith. For example, attempts to coerce people into behaving a certain way or studies designed to make me a winner and you a loser are inconsistent (I believe) with a gospel of love and grace, as are business books based in the profit motive. They are inappropriate because we in the church cannot, I believe, work from a logic of accumulation without succumbing to selfish motivations. On the other hand, there are a number of very helpful studies from secular sources that discuss how groups interact with their leaders and how groups can be mobilized to do good in the world. For example, Chris Argyris's studies of the fears that prevent leaders from learning are clearly secular in that he studied businessmen who were trying to get ahead in the world.[45] But they have strongly influenced my work, as a look at the notes will easily reveal. I felt quite comfortable using the studies because the fears he discovers illustrate a deeply theological point about how fear keeps us from God. Indeed, David Nygren, a priest who studied nuns, later confirmed the point.[46] So, I have been quite selective in which sources I thought would apply to the religious context and which ones are inappropriate for understanding congregations. But what I think is legitimate is not as important as what you the reader think is legitimate. I can have rigorous guidelines for

> Legitimacy exists in the eye of the beholder.

determining which sources are legitimate for understanding religious organizations, but if you do not agree with my assessment, the work that I do will have no credibility. I am not the arbiter of this book's legitimacy; you are. Legitimacy exists in the eye of the beholder.

Transgressing the bounds of legitimacy can be painful, even if the sin only exists in another person's mind. Let me give you an example. I once used the phrase "rule of thumb" in the title of an essay.[47] Not long after it was published, I received a scathing letter from a professor at another school. She explained that the phrase "rule of thumb" derived from a barbaric law that determined the size of a stick that a husband could legally use to beat his wife. So long as the stick was narrower than a thumbs-width, then a husband could beat his wife with impunity. The letter denounced me in the strongest terms for advocating violence toward women. She said it called my whole article into question—that is, it de-legitimated my work—even though the topic of the article was not related to violence or feminism. I was, of course, aghast. On the one hand, I felt quite defensive because I did not know the derivation of the term and certainly did not mean to indicate by my use of it that I advocated violence toward women. On the other hand, I wanted to correct whatever mistake I had made. So I called the editor of the journal where the article appeared because I did not want him to be tarred with the same brush. He explained to me that the situation was more complicated than I thought. The story about the derivation of the term was, it turned out, an urban myth. *The Oxford English Dictionary*, he said, showed a derivation that went back to the Middle Ages. I looked it up. He was right. The *OED* suggested that the phrase came from woodworking (where carpenters used their thumbs to measure) or perhaps from art (because artists often held up a thumb to align and measure distant objects).[48] He also sent me references to a William Safire article describing not only the derivation of the term but also the source of the apparent confusion.[49] It was clear after I'd done the research that the phrase never derived from abusive relationships.

What was I to do, then, with this letter and the defensive embarrassment it created in me? This is where an understanding of legitimacy becomes particularly important. I realized that the term had lost its legitimacy for an important segment of the population—academic feminists. Many of the people who were going to be reading my work or listening to me talk would take my use of the phrase as a sign that I had no sympathy for the concerns of feminism. It did not matter that the logic they used was flawed. I was going to be judged by that logic either way. I decided that I had no choice but to accept that the term had been de-legitimated and to act accordingly. I wrote an apologetic letter to the person who had angrily denounced me. I explained that I did not intend to advocate violence toward women and made sure she got her apology. When I did it at the time, I felt a bit self-righteous—like I was condescending to accommodate her ignorance. That was, of course, my wounded pride speaking. With hindsight, I realize that I had good reason to apologize. The term had indeed been de-legitimated within an important population. And those folks who said that my using the term demonstrated my ignorance were right to the extent that I did not know the debate about the term. I still feel tempted to claim a "righteous indignation" over the way I was "unfairly condemned." But I know that feeling is really just a camouflaged attempt to soothe my wounded pride. The phrase has been de-legitimated. If I use it, I have to accept the consequences.[50] But I don't get to complain. Legitimacy is, as I said, in the eye of the beholder.[51]

Understanding legitimacy is crucial to understanding sensemaking. We've already said that people who encounter a new situation can either accept a standard interpretation or create a new one. And that's directly related to legitimacy because it's another way of saying that people can either accept a pre-legitimated interpretation of a situation or they can legitimate a new one. The tool kit of cultural meanings that Swidler discussed is filled with these pre-legitimated interpretations. For example, when we look at Mindy's daily ritual, we can come up with a number of ways to make sense of it that draw on well-established interpretations. We can use the "precocious teen" interpretation, the "theological-error" interpretation, or the "God-as-projection-of-parents" interpretation. Each one resonates because it taps into stories every pastor has heard and scenes we have each seen at one time or another. I don't have to explain, for example, that sometimes people project parental relationships onto God. Most people who read this book will already have heard the idea and will have accepted (or rejected[52]) its veracity. In other words, its legitimacy is already established.[53]

And each pre-legitimated interpretation has a prescribed action that comes with it. It would not *make sense* to treat a precocious teen like a heretic—nor to treat a heretic like a precocious teen. When we adopt a

> Every time a leader wants to create transforming change, that leader will have to initiate a legitimation process to help people make sense of the new reality.

pre-legitimated interpretation, it usually comes with an established course of action.

It is easy to tell people to use only cultural resources that have legitimacy. Unfortunately, Christian leaders often experience situations where none of the pre-legitimated interpretations will work. So the question becomes, how do interpretations and courses of action get legitimated in the first place? This is a crucial question because change requires making new meaning and such new meaning often means legitimating new interpretations. Indeed, legitimation is the process of constructing new meaning. In other words, every time a leader wants to create transforming change, that leader will have to initiate a legitimation process to help people make sense of the new reality that the leader is creating.

The most common way to attain legitimacy is by a process scholars call "isomorphism."[54] It is, in short, the tendency for cultural objects to look similar to one another (isomorphic means "having the same shape"). What this means, then, is that resources and ideas gain legitimacy when they look like other things that are already legitimate.[55] This isomorphism tends to happen in one of three ways. First, there is normative isomorphism, which occurs when there are norms or rules that require legitimate objects to look similar. When a preacher stands in a pulpit, wears a black robe, and reads from a prepared text, we tend to think of that as a legitimate way to preach—even if the content is insipid and the delivery uninspiring. It still looks like a sermon should look. Second, there is coercive isomorphism, which occurs when there are significant negative consequences for looking different or significant incentives to conform. Some denominations, for example, enforce a tithe. They only allow members to be leaders in the congregation if they give a tenth of their income. They enforce this behavior, which means that anyone who aspires to leadership will conform. And, third, there is mimetic isomorphism, which is the tendency for an object to attain legitimacy by copying another object that already has legitimacy.[56] This happens, for instance, when one congregation copies ideas that they picked up from other (presumably successful) churches. The common theme is that the way to legitimate some new cultural object is to make it look like some other object that already has legitimacy.

For example, I see a number of candidates for Presbyterian ministry because I serve on my presbytery's Committee on Preparation for Ministry (CPM). Each candidate must write a one-page "statement of faith" before we will approve the candidate for ordination. These statements tend to look very similar (i.e., they are isomorphic). They tend to cover the same topics and often to use similar words or phrases. This is no accident. We provide to candidates a bank of models for what a statement looks like (mimetic isomorphism). Most begin with a phrase like, "I believe in one triune God . . ." and then they go on to cover topics such as Jesus, the Holy Spirit, the Bible, the Church, the Sacraments, and Eschatology. Students who deviate from this norm meet resistance (normative isomorphism) or can be held back from ordination (coercive isomorphism). One candidate introduced his statement by saying, "I could write the Apostles' Creed but that would not help you know what I believe so I've tried to explain my faith by giving analogies." He then wrote statements like, "I believe the Church is like . . ." or "I believe that Baptism is like . . ." The CPM agreed that the statement was very thoughtful and probably one of the most impressive the committee had seen. But it took a long time to reach that conclusion. The very strength of the statement (the fact that it did not look like others the committee was used to seeing) made it hard for the CPM to accept it at first. It did not follow the unwritten rules (normative isomorphism). In a similar way, I worry because we see lots of candidates who use all the right words—it seems that they all say that a sacrament is an "outward sign of an inward grace." But we cannot always tell that the candidates understand what the words mean. We ask them to explain their statements. But I am sure there are students who slip by because we did not ask the questions that would reveal the student's ignorance. Our job on the CPM is to determine if the student has written a legitimate statement of faith. The absence, however, of clear standards for legitimacy means that we often judge candidates not on merit but on their ability to match the statements of faith we have already decided are legitimate. That's isomorphism.

There is another example of isomorphism that is almost ubiquitous in congregations. It happens when congregations face a problem that they do not really know how to solve—problems like a generational divide, or changing demographics, or (the most common one) declining membership.

In such situations, congregations tend to copy methods that they think have been successful in other churches. This is how, say, seeker-sensitive services became so common. They were pioneered at congregations that had very specific (nearly unique) institutional circumstances. The right people on staff, the right demographics in the neighborhood, and the right timing often combined to make these programs work. And once they worked (or once people believed that they worked), others tried to copy the programs. But the congregations who copy them often do not have the personnel, the facilities, the demographics, or the timing to make it work.[57] So the programs appear to accomplish more than they can deliver.

But that's the point. Appearing to address the situation is often enough to avert a congregational crisis. So here's the irony of isomorphism. Because one congregation's circumstances differ so widely from another's, copying what others have done may not be the best way to address a difficult problem, but it is usually the best way for a congregation to feel that it is addressing a difficult problem. Conversely, pursuing a strategy tailored to a congregation's unique circumstances may be a better way to address a difficult problem, but it will likely do little to ease the congregational anxiety that the crisis created. Copying other church's ideas may placate people long enough for them to get so comfortable that they stop seeing the problem, and choosing not to copy may increase people's anxiety so much that they stop trying to change things. (Can you hear the echoes of "failing people's expectations at a rate they can stand"?) Legitimacy is important because people tend to follow pre-legitimated avenues to action.[58]

> Leaders provide a theological framework that enables others to make their own spiritual meaning.

How then do pastors make spiritual meaning? It turns out they do not. Ministers do not make meaning for other people.[59] Instead leaders provide a theological framework that enables others to make their own spiritual meaning. Each person has to construct meaning for himself or herself. The pastor can only provide legitimated cultural tools—theological categories and spiritual vocabulary—that people can use as they each make their own meaning.

In this first part of the book, I have described the process that people use to make sense of situations in their world. I argued that pastors lead by help-ing God's people use theological categories and frameworks to make spiri-tual sense. Part 2 will show how leaders can shape that meaning-making process and why such a shaping is leadership. But in between, there are two important points that bridge parts 1 and 2. The first is that a leader's goal can and should be to help people to internalize the habit of using theo-logical categories to make sense of their world. And the second is a caveat that says that pastors cannot control the meaning that people make.

Part 1 broke the process of sensemaking into component parts—parts that deal with expectations, with selecting from culture's repertoire of meaning, with comparing stories, and with following pre-legitimated avenues to action. It is tempting then to conclude from this discussion that making meaning is a long, arduous process. Yet the truth is just the opposite. It happens in an instant. When I saw that little lost girl in the grocery store hugging her father, I knew instantly what had happened. And when I saw those suspects surrendering to the police, I breathed eas-ily without having to go through a complicated process. It was almost instinctive. We have divided the process into constituent parts so that we can understand it. But we cannot lose sight of the fact that sensemaking comes in an instant.

This has huge implications for the work of leadership. A Christian leader's goal must be to enable people to internalize a theological frame-work that allows them to make spiritual sense of the world instanta-neously. We have already seen how quickly impressions are formed. And these first impressions often become the logic that people use to organize the data that they encounter. Unless those theological categories leap immediately to mind, people are often well along a secular path before they think about the spiritual implications of a situation. And we have seen how difficult it is to go back once a person has started along a par-ticular path of interpretation. Thus a leader's eventual goal will be to help a person internalize the theological categories that are the building blocks of making spiritual meaning.

It is also important to note the limitations of leadership. Pastors can only influence; they cannot control the meaning another person makes. Each person has access to her or his own repertoire of cultural meanings. I mentioned earlier that one pastor who read this story interpreted the police car scene very differently than I did. Her experience in life led her to conclude that the police cannot always be trusted. So she asked me a lot of questions about the situation. But no matter what I said in response, she could not shake the feeling that the police were likely overreacting to the situation. Neither of us will ever really know what happened that day. But the most salient part of the story for her was not anything I said. It was her years of experience. That experience ensured that she and I would interpret the situation differently.

The same thing happens when a pastor preaches a sermon. No matter how careful the pastor is to set up a particular interpretation, he cannot control the ways that the experiences of the individual congregants will attach new meanings to the sermon. Every preacher has had this experience. I have been the preacher and I have been the congregant who wandered astray of the preacher's intended meaning. I preached not long ago on a passage from Galatians. It was more of a doctrinal sermon than one designed to elicit an emotional response. At the door after the service, one misty-eyed woman clutched my hand earnestly and told me how much the sermon meant to her. It turned out that one of the illustrations I had used made her think of her recently deceased husband. And somehow the way that I told the story made her realize anew how he continued to live in her memory. Now, that was not my intent at all. I could never know the connotations that she would attach to that story.[60] But the meaning of the sermon for her that day was that her husband remained with her. I have also been the congregant who wanders away from the meaning that the preacher intends. Any mention of Proverbs 3:5-6 ("Trust in the LORD with all your heart") makes me think of my great-grandmother. I invariably have her in my mind when a sermon mentions that passage. Leaders cannot control the meaning that people assign to a situation because we cannot restrict the repertoire of cultural meanings from which people will build their interpretations.

Perhaps the best way to end this discussion of making spiritual meaning is to illustrate how the words of Jesus in the Sermon on the Mount illustrate the lessons that a leader can learn from this discussion of making spiritual meaning. In Matthew 5, Jesus repeatedly used the formula, "You have heard it said . . . but I say to you . . . " Let me exegete that passage by pointing out the leadership lessons that we can learn from Jesus' words.

1. Change people's expectations

The first thing Jesus did was to change people's expectations—both the expectations that they attached to the Law and the expectations that they attached to the Messiah. Up until Jesus, the dominant view of the Law allowed people to interpret an implicit bargain embedded in the Law. Keeping the Law entitled someone to the good gifts of God's blessing. At the heart of the bargain was an assumption that a person could keep the Law. And keeping the Law was defined by the rules and interpretations that the Jewish traditions had created for applying the Law to daily life. Jesus wanted to change the expectation that it was possible for a person to keep the Law by showing the people that God maintained a much higher standard for obedience than the Pharisees did. He wanted them to see that it was impossible to keep the Law. He said that even insulting another person made one as culpable as the person who commits murder. The Pharisees' teachings had led them to expect that obedience was the best way to enter God's favor. Jesus exploded their expectations so that they would be open to an alternative view. Instead of mastering the Law and demanding from God the prize that comes with obedience, Jesus opened the door to seeking forgiveness as the path to God. He changed their expectations.

2. Draw from a different repertoire of cultural resources

His followers interpreted Jesus as a rabbi. That is why, for example, people approached him with the title, "good teacher." And part of being a rabbi was mastering the repertoire of Jewish stories and sayings. Indeed, the accepted way to carry on debate about a text's meaning was to compare the various interpretations that were already a part of the tradition. This was the repertoire of meaning from which people expected Jesus to draw. And this was the repertoire the Pharisees used. But Jesus did not do that. He pointed back instead to the Hebrew Scriptures.

In so doing Jesus also reinterpreted the meaning of his own identity. Some thought of him as a teacher, others a prophet. Some even expected that he would be the political leader who would restore the fortunes of a captive nation. But Jesus did not choose to fit any of those expectations. At the same time, he did not reject the tradition wholeheartedly. When John the Baptist sends word asking about his cousin's identity, Jesus answers with a quote from Isaiah 61. "The Spirit of the Lord is upon me, because he has anointed me to bring good news to the poor. He sent me to proclaim release to the captives and recovery of sight to the blind, to let the oppressed go free, to proclaim the year of the Lord's favor" (Luke 4:18-19). He transformed the meaning of Messiah and shifted people's expectations by drawing on a different set of cultural resources to make sense of his identity.

3. Weave these resources together using a narrative structure

The message of judgment at the beginning of the Sermon on the Mount becomes a message of hope by the sermon's end. Jesus reshapes the people's understanding of the Law at the beginning of the Sermon so that it is clear that they have no hope of attaining righteousness under the Law. But then he offers the good news by the end of the next chapter. He tells the people not to succumb to fear because God cares for them. He offers them an image of hope. "Ask, and it will be given you; search, and you will find . . . " (Matt. 7:7; Luke 11:9). And then he paints a simple little picture that allows them to paint themselves into the story. "Is there anyone among you who, if your child asks for bread, will give a stone? Or if the child asks for a fish, will give a snake? If you then, who are evil, know how to give good gifts to your children, how much more will your Father in heaven give good things to those who ask him!" (Matt. 7:9-11). It is a simple narrative structure. God is your Father in heaven. God is a better Father than you will ever be. You can take care of children. So we can conclude that God will take care of you. And then to tie all his teachings together, he tells the parable of the man who built his house on the sand. The Law is shifting sand. But the love of your Father in heaven is solid rock. Which one will make a reliable foundation for your life? The narrative structure allows even a child to understand that the sands cannot be trusted. Only the love of the God who gives good gifts to his children, only that God can be trusted. The story encapsulates and weaves together the Sermon's themes.

4. Make sure that a clear set of actions is the natural consequence of the story-shaped interpretation

The consequences of failing to keep the Law are quite clear. The punishment for murder is death. The punishment for adultery is death. And lest anyone misunderstand Jesus' intentions and think that he wants to sweep away the Law, he explains clearly how he views the Law. "Anyone who breaks one of the least of these commandments and teaches others to do the same will be called least in the kingdom of heaven, but whoever practices and teaches these commands will be called great in the kingdom of heaven. For I tell you that unless your righteousness surpasses that of the Pharisees and the teachers of the law, you will certainly not enter the kingdom of heaven" (Matt. 5:19-20 NIV). The clear implication of Jesus' teaching is that God desires a different kind of obedience than the one that the Pharisees proclaim. The Pharisees, of course, felt the barb of his critique. They knew exactly what he was saying. And they hated him for it. Instead of smug obedience to a hollow standard, Jesus called for the kind of love that loves enemies and goes the extra mile. It was quite clear what Jesus wanted his followers to do.

5. Whenever possible, tap into pre-legitimated pathways

Jesus did not, however, create his message out of whole cloth. He did not need to explain concepts like Law and prophets. He built on the foundation that was already there. The people knew that God could and did have the right to define the parameters of righteousness. They knew that about murder, adultery, and oppression. He simply took their understanding to a new level. He did not have to eliminate their categories. Instead he redefined them. That made it easy for people to figure out what the next step of faithfulness looked like. When he called them hypocrites, they knew exactly what he meant and what special judgment God reserved for those who spoke one thing but did another. The Sermon on the Mount uses many pre-legitimated pathways.

6. Sometimes a leader must legitimate fresh interpretations

There are, however, crucial moments when Jesus introduces ideas that are new to his hearers. They have never heard someone speak in such intimate ways about God. There are moments when the Hebrew prophets infer such intimacy—such as when Isaiah quotes God as saying to Israel, "Can a mother forget the baby at her breast and have no compassion on the child she has borne? Though she may forget, I will not forget you!" (Isaiah 49:15 NIV). The intimacy in Isaiah is, however, only an analogy. Jesus makes that intimacy plain calling God, "your Father in heaven" and saying that this father will give good gifts to his children. This presumes an intimacy that must have been jarring to a people that regularly replaced the proper name of God with a placeholder, "the LORD." The Pharisees revered God so much that they did not call God by name. But Jesus used a family name to emphasize the intimate care that God promises to give those who seek God's righteousness. Jesus did not rely solely on pre-legitimated categories. At key moments, Jesus legitimated fresh interpretations.

7. The goal is to enable people to internalize the new expectations and interpretations

We often misuse the word *teacher* to describe someone whose only goal is to convey information. Jesus wanted people to internalize his teaching to the point that it became the primary lens that the person used to interpret the world. It is not enough simply to acknowledge that insults are as bad as murder or that God calls us to meet insults with love. All that does is allow a person to move in an informed way to personal destruction. That does no one any good. The ultimate goal of Jesus' teaching is to change people's lives. And the only way that can happen is for it to shape the outlook with which they approach the world. Think, for example, of Jesus' admonition at the end of the Sermon on the Mount to "turn the other cheek." He is referring to a decision that each of us makes in a split second. A person reacts to a slap instinctively. There is no time for careful consideration. In the moment I am slapped, I have either internalized Jesus' teaching or I have not. Either it has changed my instantaneous reaction or it has not.

This is a crucial lesson for leaders who wish to make spiritual meaning. It is all too tempting to see the teaching task as didactic rather than formative. The goal of a leader has to be formation. It is to create a perspective for interpreting the world. And that cannot happen in a single lesson. It comes only from repeated lessons moving in the same direction. People glimpse new perspectives slowly and in pieces. They need to experiment with a new outlook on the world and play with it before it can become their own. The ultimate goal of sensemaking is to enable someone to internalize a new way of interpreting the world.

8. Even Jesus cannot control the meaning that people make

The message of part 1 of this book is easy to misunderstand. It is possible to see these last few points as so many easy steps that guarantee a promised outcome. But meaning making does not work that way. Even Jesus could not control the meaning that his hearers made. The Pharisees took the exact opposite meaning from the one Jesus intended. And even Jesus' closest followers did not really understand the implications of his message after three years with him. The meaning-making leader must understand that no person can make meaning for someone else. All a leader can do is to create categories and interpretations that she hopes other people will choose to adopt for themselves.

That, of course, leads naturally to another question. How can a leader construct meaning so that her hearers are likely to adopt that meaning as their own? That is the subject for part 2.

Notes

1. This and other descriptions of the Almond Springs church come from a multi-episode case study that describes a year in the life of the fictional congregation (available on-line at www.christianleaders.org). For a description of how the cases were created and an explanation for why this type of fictional case study can be more appropriate for teaching leadership, see Scott Cormode, "Using Computers in Theological Education: Rules of Thumb," *Theological Education* 36, no. 1 (Autumn 1999): 101–16 and a review of the multi-episode case study in Michael Jenkins, "Theological Dot Education: A Review of the Almond Springs Web Site, www.christianleaders.org," *Teaching Theology and Religion*, 5, no. 1 (February 2002).

2. Let me be clear about my use of language. Throughout this part I make generalizing statements like "people make sense of a situation by . . . " or "we draw on cultural resources . . . " I do not mean to say that all people in all places and in every situation think this way. That would be absurd. My intent, instead, is to make a generalizing statement about how people act under "normal" conditions. So when you encounter these generalizing statements, take them as a cue to mentally insert words like "normally" or "as a rule" or "on the whole." It would be stylistically awkward to include such qualifying statements in every paragraph. But it would be misleading to let the plain meaning of the sentences stand.

3. These frameworks can take many forms. For example, the philosopher Alasdair MacIntyre argues that making sense of a situation involves placing it in a larger story. In order to demonstrate the power of a larger framework to shape the meaning of a situation, he invites readers, in the words of Brad J. Kallenberg, to imagine an odd scene and then notice how we make sense of it. "Imagine that a woman approaches you at a bus stop and says, 'The name of the common wild duck is *histrionicus histrionicus histrionicus*.' Now, what would you make of this person? Truth is, you can't make anything of her, or of her action,

without more information. Her act is completely unintelligible. But now suppose it becomes known that this woman is a librarian, and she has mistaken you for the person who earlier had asked for the Latin name of the common wild duck. We can now understand her action because it has been put into a context. The contexts that make sense out of human action are *stories* or *narratives*. To explain an action is simply to provide the story that gives the act its context." The framework provides the interpretative cues that give a situation its meaning. Kallenberg, "The Master Argument of MacIntyre's *After Virtue*," in *Virtues and Practices in the Christian Tradition: Christian Ethics after MacIntyre*, eds. Nancey Murphy, Brad J. Kallenberg, and Mark Thiessen Nation (Notre Dame, Ind.: University of Notre Dame Press, 1997), 22–23.

4. The sociologist Robert Wuthnow puts it this way: "Stories help us encapsulate experience so we can remember it." He then references the work of Roger Schank, a cognitive scientist whose ideas about just-in-time learning and the role of narrative in creating a longing to learn were instrumental in shaping the form of the Almond Springs episodes. Robert Wuthnow, "Stories to Live By," *Theology Today* 49, no. 3 (October 1992): 307; on Schank, see Roger C. Schank and Chip Cleary, *Engines for Education* (Hillsdale, N.J.: Lawrence Erlbaum Associates, 1995); on Schank's influence on Almond Springs, see Cormode, "Using Computers."

5. Note that the phrases "making meaning," "meaning making," "sensemaking," and "making sense" are interchangeable. References to "sensemaking" and "making sense" refer to Karl Weick's seminal work in organizational psychology. See his book *The Social Psychology of Organizing* (New York: McGraw-Hill, 1979 [1969]) for an introduction to his ideas. To explore them in depth, see a compendium of his essays and articles, published as Karl E. Weick, *Making Sense of the Organization* (Oxford: Blackwell Publishers, 2001); a more accessible approach to his ideas can be found in Diane L. Coutu, "Sense and Reliability: A Conversation with Celebrated Psychologist Karl E. Weick," *Harvard Business Review* (April 2003): 3–7.

6. Some readers have pointed out that their experience or their context would not lead them to such an expectation. Even in a sleepy suburban town, they would immediately ask questions about race and ethnicity. One reader, for example, immediately wondered if the occupants of the car were Hispanic. When I said one was Hispanic and the other African American, she asked if perhaps instead of being dangerous criminals, these two could be victims of an establishment that increasingly overreacts to the presence of people who look different from themselves. I will never know. My town is so ethnically and racially diverse that overreacting police would have to detain half the cars if they were genuinely afraid of otherness. But the point of telling the story is that I set the situation in the context that made the most sense to me—just as my reader set the scene in the context that makes the most sense to her. The disparity of interpretations further reinforces the idea that the event had many possible meanings.

7. This is what MacIntyre means when he says that we make sense of our lives by placing them within larger stories, "Human actions are intelligible only with respect to stories" and "that which unifies actions…is the story of one's own life." Kallenberg, "Master Argument," 23 (see n. 3).

8. The best summary of scholarship on leadership is Alan Bryman, "Leadership in Organizations" in *Handbook of Organization Studies*, eds. Stewart R. Clegg, Cynthia Hardy, and Walter R. Nord (Thousand Oaks, Calif.: Sage Publications, 1996), 276–92. Note, I have summarized the trajectory of scholarship and in so doing have left out

milestones that others might want to emphasize. Indeed, I skipped entirely the so-called "contingency theories" that were popular in and around the 1970s. The meaning-making approach is summarized as the "symbolic frame" in Lee G. Bolman and Terrence E. Deal, *Reframing Organizations: Artistry, Choice, and Leadership,* Second Edition (San Francisco: Jossey-Bass, 1991), 243–308; another way to approach the trajectory question is to look at "what constituents expect of leaders." James M. Kouzes and Barry Z. Posner take this tack in chapter 2 of *The Leadership Challenge: How to Keep Getting Extraordinary Things Done in Organizations* (San Francisco: Jossey-Bass, 1995), 19–31.

9. Bryman, "Leadership in Organizations," 276, 277, 280; cf. Linda Smirich and Gareth Morgan, "Leadership: The Management of Meaning," *Journal of Applied Behavioral Studies* 18 (1982): 257–73; Jeffrey Pfeffer, "Management as Symbolic Action: The Creation and Maintenance of Organizational Paradigms," *Research in Organizational Behavior* 3 (1981): 1–52; Jeffrey Pfeffer, "The Ambiguity of Leadership," *Academy of Management Review* 2 (1977): 104-119; Linda Lambert, "Toward a Theory of Constructivist Leadership," in *The Constructivist Leader* ed. Linda Lambert (New York: Teachers' College Press, 1995), 28–51; on organizational culture, the standard work is Edgar Schein, *Organizational Culture and Leadership* (San Francisco: Jossey-Bass, 1992).

10. James MacGregor Burns, *Leadership* (New York: Harper & Row, 1978); note that, as scholars began to explore Burns's distinction between transactional and transforming leadership, the nomenclature evolved so that we now talk of "transformational" leadership; cf. Bryman, "Leadership in Organizations," 280.

11. Wilfred H. Drath and Charles J. Palus, *Making Common Sense: Leadership as Meaning-making in a Community of Practice* (Greensboro, N.C.: Center for Creative Leadership, 1994 [2001]), 3, 4, 9.

12. Max DePree, *Leadership Is an Art* (New York: Doubleday, 1989), 11.

13. The study correlated the first impressions with other groups that watched a very long segment of teaching. The results did not change. First impressions yielded the same consensus on teaching as came from watching a long session. Malcolm Gladwell, "The New-Boy Network: What Do Job Interviews Really Tell Us," *The New Yorker* (May 29, 2000): 68–86.

14. Gladwell, "New-Boy Network."

15. This tendency for a person to be deceived by their own expectation is one of the many reasons why Chris Argyris emphasizes "hypothesis testing." Indeed, he believes that the only way to test a hypothesis is to use a different set of data from the one that generated the idea in the first place. Thus, for example, Charlotte walked away from this Worship Committee meeting believing that Margo was uninterested in the preaching of the church. That was her hypothesis, one that turned out to be wrong. But there is no way she could test that hypothesis simply by reflecting on the meeting, according to Chris Argyris. Since she used the meeting to generate the hypothesis, she would have to find another situation to test the hypothesis. In other words, Argyris teaches us that the meaning we make can easily deceive us, so we have to hold onto it loosely until we find some way to figure out if we have interpreted correctly. Argyris explains the importance of hypothesis testing in article form in "Teaching Smart People How to Learn," *Harvard Business Review* (May-June 1991): 5–15, and in book form in *Knowledge for Action: A Guide to Overcoming Barriers to Organizational Change* (San Francisco: Jossey-Bass, 1993) and *Flawed Advice and the Management Trap: How Managers Can Know When They're Getting Good Advice and When They're Not* (New York: Oxford University Press, 2000).

16. Understanding the pain that failed expectations cause is, of course, only the first step.

17. Ronald A. Heifetz, *Leadership Without Easy Answers* (Cambridge: Harvard University Press, 1994), 83.

18. Argyris, "Teaching Smart People How to Learn"; cf. Anita Farber-Robertson, *Learning While Leading: Increasing Your Effectiveness in Ministry* (Washington, D.C.: The Alban Institute, 2000), which attempts to translate some of Argyris's key ideas to the congregational realm.

19. Pastors reading this will recognize the dilemma and each no doubt has her way of dealing with it. I do two things to combat my tendency to espouse more hospitality than I deliver. I tell my students this story up front so that I am not setting their expectations too high. And I have worked out a script I follow when I find myself giving someone short shrift. I tell them that I am in the middle of something and/or distracted (which is usually the reason for my inattention) and then I ask them if we can make an appointment for an alternative time. Usually this works. Every once in awhile, however, a student's reaction tells me that later will not work. Seeing their need usually is enough to focus my attention. But, I must admit, I have a way to go before I feel great about how well I live up to my espoused theory of hospitality.

20. Another name for unspoken expectations is "assumptions." But I am avoiding that phrasing because there is such a negative connotation to the word "assume." (We all know the aphorism about what assuming does.) Leaders cannot be in a position of embarrassing people. If we tell people we are surfacing assumptions, there are people who will feel that we are blaming them for having unspoken expectations. We want to avoid any language that encourages defensiveness or blame.

21. On competing commitments, see Robert Kegan and Lisa Laskow Lahey, *How the Way We Talk Can Change the Way We Work: Seven Languages for Transformation* (San Francisco: Jossey-Bass, 2001), 47–66.

22. Weick had in mind the ways that organizations think when he wrote that. But, as Swidler will show us, the concept applies as well to individuals. "Organizations talk to themselves," Weick has written, "in order to clarify their surroundings and learn more about them." Weick, "Enactment Processes in Organizations," reprinted in *Making Sense of the Organization*, esp. 189–91 (see n. 5).

23. A classic overview of the notion of culture is Wendy Griswold, *Cultures and Societies in a Changing World* (Thousand Oaks, Calif.: Sage Publications, 1993); on the ways that the symbolic elements of culture get shaped by the systems that create them, see Richard A. Peterson and N. Anand, "The Production of Culture Perspective," *Annual Review of Sociology* 30 (Palo Alto, Calif.: Annual Reviews, 2004): 311–34; on the application of this production of culture perspective to religious elements of culture, see Wuthnow, *Producing the Sacred: An Essay on Public Religion* (Urbana, Ill.: University of Illinois Press, 1994).

24. This quick and dirty definition comes from Michael Schudson, "How culture works: Perspectives from media studies on the efficacy of symbols," *Theory and Society* 18 (1989): 153. Most contemporary definitions of culture eventually refer back to Clifford Geertz's seminal work on *The Interpretation of Cultures* (New York: Basic Books, 1973).

25. It is important to note another sociological debate that we will not take the time to explore here. Some scholars believe that culture is but a shadow cast by the social structure, where structure refers both to sociodemographic categories (such as race, gender, and

class) and to the deep patterns that configure those categories. This book takes the approach, summarized by Robert Wuthnow, that "culture is not simply a reflection of social structure but contains an elaborate internal structure of its own that borrows from the social world, textualizes that material, and in the process transforms it." Wuthnow, "Introduction: New Directions in the Empirical Study of Cultural Codes," in Robert Wuthnow, ed., *Vocabularies of Public Life: Empirical Essays in Symbolic Structure* (London: Routledge, 1992), 9.

26. The most widely quoted summary of this view is Ann Swidler, "Culture in Action: Symbols and Strategies," *American Sociological Review* 15 (April 1986): 273–86.

27. I should note that proclaiming forgiveness and hope is not the only way to respond pastorally to Gary. Some readers have argued that the grace Charlotte proclaims is too "cheap," to use Dietrich Bonhoeffer's phrase. They believe that there needs to be some kind of renewal process before Gary is ready to be accepted for baptism. Others argue that his years of self-imposed exile and conscience-racked striving mitigate against cheap grace. The important point this caveat makes is that the most pastoral response is not necessarily the least painful one.

28. Ann Swidler, *Talk of Love: How Culture Matters* (Chicago: University of Chicago Press, 2000), 24, 25.

29. Swidler, *Talk of Love.*

30. Notice, then, that the culture of Christianity becomes a repertoire of repertoires.

31. Chris Argyris has shown that defensive reasoning is prevalent when people either do not want to acknowledge a weakness or mistake, or when they use their strengths to hide their weaknesses. The problem with defensive reasoning is that it prevents people from learning from their mistakes and thus dooms them to repeat them continually. Argyris, "Teaching Smart People (see n. 15)."

32. His politician's repertoire created a strange calculus when it came to the truth. It was more complicated than the stereotype that politicians tell lies to get their way. He believed so much in the importance of face-to-face understanding that he would agree to things (say, funding a new project) without thinking through the future implications. Only later, when someone pointed out the collateral costs of the deal he had made (say, that he had already spent the money he intended for the new project), would he back out of the deal. But, even then he did not see it as backing out of the deal because he did not consider that the implications of changing his mind would be that someone would see him as going back on his word. His politician's repertoire created for him expectations that said that any agreement was subject to future amendment.

33. Swidler, 30.

34. I recognize that most ministers and therapists would resist labeling themselves as experts. But I use that term because it is exactly the role that the couple wanted from them. They saw themselves as seeking advice from experts in the same way that a person with a disease seeks the advice of a doctor. Their intent was to heal their marriage.

35. Swidler, 17.

36. Swidler, 34.

37. She also said, "deductive logic is not central to the organization of cultural systems." Swidler, *Talk of Love*, 188, 189.

38. Swidler, 29, 30.

39. Let me say from the beginning that, because of the controversial nature of homosexuality in the churches, people sometimes get sidetracked by this situation. Some liber-

als will be outraged because they believe Margo to be homophobic. Some conservatives will say to themselves that Margo is making a legitimate point. In the end, you will see that your stance on the homosexuality question does not need to influence how you interpret the example.

40. I am not saying that congregations should be unsympathetic. But what I am saying is that they (or at least their leaders) should be clear about why they are making a decision. We sometimes construct convoluted rationales to justify decisions that really did not have anything to do with rationality. If we make a decision for sympathetic reasons, we should be aware that we are doing it.

41. Note the irrelevance of the truth to her reasoning. Darien was not gay. But she believed him to be gay. So she interpreted Herb as if he were being compared to a gay candidate. Her perception created its own reality for her.

42. Mary E. Hess, *Engaging Technology in Theological Education: All That We Can't Leave Behind* (Lanham, Md.: Rowman & Littlefield, 2005).

43. One of the pastors who commented on this section pointed out an important irony in the way that the congregation made sense of the interview. They did not learn from their mistake with the previous choir director, this pastor said. The biggest problem with the earlier director was that she was not a good team member. Yet nowhere in the debate do the committees evaluate the candidates by comparing how they would function as members of a team. This pastor concluded by saying, "You can teach theology; you can't change a personality." Her point is, ironically, that sympathetic identification may well have led the congregation to make a better decision than the one that it reached by trying to be objective.

44. This definition of legitimacy comes from W. Richard Scott's standard textbook, *Organizations: Rational, Natural, and Open Systems, Third Edition* (Englewood Cliffs, N.J.: Prentice-Hall, 1992 [1981]), 307. Other organizational scholars would use slightly different definitions. But each would explain legitimacy in terms of what the cultural rules define as appropriate. The lineage of the term traces back to Talcott Parsons's emphasis on values. See, especially, Jeffrey Pfeffer and Gerald Salancik, *The External Control of Organizations: A Resource Dependence Perspective* (Stanford, Calif.: Stanford Business Classics, 2003 [1978]), esp. 193–202; W. Richard Scott, "Unpacking Institutional Arguments," in Walter W. Powell and Paul J. DiMaggio, *The New Institutionalism in Organizational Analysis* (Chicago: University of Chicago Press, 1991), 164–82.

45. The best place to investigate Argyris's work is, "Teaching Smart People (see no. 15)"; cf. Anita Farber-Robertson, *Learning while Leading* (see no. 18).

46. David J. Nygren, Miriam D. Ukeritis, David C. McClelland, and Julia L. Hickman, "Outstanding Leadership in Nonprofit Organizations: Leadership Competencies in Roman Catholic Religious Orders," *Nonprofit Management & Leadership* 4, no. 4 (Summer 1994): 375–91.

47. Scott Cormode, "Using Computers in Theological Education: Rules of Thumb."

48. *A New English Dictionary on Historical Principles* (now known as the *Oxford English Dictionary*) Volume VII (Oxford: Clarendon Press, 1914): 885.

49. William Safire, "On Language; Misrule of Thumb," *New York Times* (January 25, 1998); Safire quotes a September 1994 article in the *Journal of Legal Education* and details how an English judge made a remark to the effect that the rule of thumb applied to spousal abuse in 1782 and was publicly ridiculed for it. He notes that the etymology of the term traces further back than the eighteenth century and that the only legal use of the term

with relation to spousal abuse was severely and publicly rejected. Safire concludes, "The idea that the rule of thumb is derived from an early form of spousal abuse is in error."

50. Some folks might question this strategy because, as one person said, "You are caving to the political correctness police." That may or may not be true. But it is irrelevant. If I use the phrase, I have to accept that some people will assign to it connotations I do not intend. I have enough battles to fight where I create misunderstanding. I don't have time to manufacture one. I'll save my cultural capital for times that I have no choice but to fail people's expectations. Here I have a choice.

51. One option, which I did not decide to follow in this case, is to reeducate the people to whom I am speaking. I can explain how and why I use the phrase before I use it. But that seems a bit pedantic. I can't stop every time I use the phrase to explain myself. The phrase is not an important one and my vocabulary will not be diminished if I refrain from using it.

52. Even rejecting an idea such as parental projection establishes its legitimacy. You may not agree with the idea. But the fact that you have to take it seriously enough to argue against it (rather than rejecting it out of hand) shows that it has veracity in some quarters. And showing veracity in some quarters is usually enough to establish first-order legitimacy.

53. Legitimacy depends on context. When a leader is speaking to an audience, the leader is only convincing if she uses resources and rationales that are legitimate to the audience. Every leader has a feel for this at some level. You don't expect teens to be convinced by references to Shakespeare nor do you expect senior citizens to be moved by an example from MTV. But I am not just talking about cultural tools that are supposed to be legitimate or that are legitimate to the speaker. For example, pastors hold Scripture in high esteem. So quoting Scripture to politicians may look good. But it likely will have as little effect on them as that Shakespearean sonnet had on hormonal teens. Likewise, a speaker who quotes something that they recently read, or tells a story conveyed by an esteemed mentor, will often compromise their own effectiveness. The speaker needs to legitimate the source before telling the story. Think, for instance, about the references that appear in this book. I cannot assume that you, the reader, have ever heard of, say, Chris Argyris. So when I quoted him earlier I introduced him as "the respected Harvard scholar Chris Argyris." Argyris is famous, but not among pastors. His name does not lend immediate credence to his words. So I tried to give him a subtle boost by how I introduced him. It takes more, however, to legitimate a source than to simply say good things about it. I did not need to do much legitimating for Argyris because you, the reader, were likely to accept his words as part of the text's argument whether you'd ever heard of him or not. But think back to the minister who is quoting Scripture to a politician (or to a teenager). The pastor is often in a position of asking the politician or the teen to change behavior based solely on the credibility of Scripture. (This kind of Scripture-as-authoritative-guide rationale is not unique to conservative Christians. Liberal Christians often make this kind of argument to political leaders. Say a pastor is advocating for justice. The pastor is likely to quote Scripture as an authoritative guide even if neither the pastor nor the politician has a theological framework that sees the Bible as inerrant or inspired.) The pastor needs to create a context where the Bible (or Jesus) has legitimacy in the moment. Or the pastor needs to find a different source to use when trying to convince an audience, a source that the audience already accepts as credible. In other words, there is a difference between my quoting Argyris in this book and a pastor quoting Scripture to a politician. And the

difference has to do with the change one hopes to engender. Someone reading a book is likely to give the book the benefit of the doubt and accept Argyris as part of a larger whole—also, his credibility is not crucial to your conceding the point that there is a disparity between what people claim to do and what they actually do. The pastor quoting Scripture to the politician faces a greater challenge because the politician does not share the pastor's primary motivation, which may well derive from seeing Scripture as God's word. It is not enough for the pastor to establish the first-order legitimacy of Scripture as an authority for someone. He must establish the second-order legitimacy of Scripture as an authority *over the politician's life*. The degree of legitimacy a speaker needs to establish has to do with how much action the speaker hopes to engender from the hearer. The more action you expect from a hearer, the greater legitimacy you need to establish.

54. Powell and DiMaggio, "Iron Cage Revisited," in *The New Institutionalism in Organizational Analysis*, 1–40; Scott Cormode, "Does Institutional Isomorphism Imply Secularization? Churches and Secular Voluntary Associations in the Turn-of-the-Century-City," in *Sacred Companies: Organizational Aspects of Religion and Religious Aspects of Organizations* (New York: Oxford University Press, 1998), 116–31.

55. I am going to expand in this section on the way that Powell and DiMaggio use "isomorphism." They use the term to apply solely to organizations and to organizational structure. I want to argue that the same process applies to any legitimated cultural objects or cultural tools. The precedent for pursuing this line of argument comes from DiMaggio's work on how the American definition of "good art" was established in the nineteenth century. Powell and DiMaggio, "Iron Cage Revisited"; Paul DiMaggio, "Cultural Entrepreneurship in Nineteenth-Century Boston," *Media, Culture, and Society* 4 (1982): 33–50.

56. For a discussion of how isomorphic legitimation helps congregations respond to inundating change, see Nancy T. Ammerman, *Congregation & Community* (New Brunswick, N.J.: Rutgers University Press, 1997), 46, 47. Ammerman talks here about how legitimacy contributes to the "survival of the similar" and the "survival of the savvy."

57. This is why it is so important to learn from failure. There is a strong sentiment among many organizational scholars that copying the success of others (i.e., mimetic isomorphism) *cannot* work. They argue that so many factors have to come together for a program to work that it is all but impossible for an outside observer (or even for an insider) to determine which of the factors contributed most to the success of the program. These scholars believe, by contrast, that less-than-successful endeavors are more educational because we often point to the moment when things started to go wrong. Their point is that eliminating known mistakes is often a far more effective way to improve than emulating perceived successes. Cf. Jeffrey Pfeffer and Robert Sutton, *The Knowing-Doing Gap* (Cambridge, Mass.: Harvard Business School Press, 2000).

58. There is one pre-legitimated avenue to action that deserves special attention because it is so powerful in Christian contexts. Practices provide a particularly poignant way to mobilize action among Christians. Practices have the weight of history behind them. They are more than means to an end; they justify themselves; they are ends unto themselves. Think of a practice such as prayer. It is more than simply a means to the end of getting God to do something. When we pray we participate in God's larger purpose for the world. It is as much about the relationship between the person and God as it is about any particular request. Indeed, it refers to a breadth of communications between people and God—anything from praise (such as Psalm 100) to anger directed at God (such as Psalm 22).

59. The fact that each person creates her own spiritual meaning is related to the organizational idea of "ambiguity." See Michael D. Cohen and James G. March, *Leadership and Ambiguity* (Boston: Harvard Business School Press, 1974). It also explains the importance of competing commitments, which derive not only from the fact that different people assign divergent meaning to the same event but also from the fact that the same person often entertains competing interpretations within her or his own understanding of an event or situation.

60. We can, however, anticipate that there are certain passages or interpretations that have the potential to conjure strong feelings for some people. For example, in that same sermon, I discussed the biblical image that we are adopted children of God. I could anticipate that a discussion of adoption would have larger emotional connotations for some segment of the congregation. So I could monitor how I discussed adoption and could be sensitive to the implications that it might elicit. There are also particular passages that have been used so many times in very specific contexts that they are likely to conjure memories associated with that context. For instance, any discussion of Psalm 23 is likely to call to mind a funeral for someone. There are times that we can anticipate that our interpretations will elicit collateral feelings and interpretations.

PART TWO

LEADERS SHAPE MEANING

Christian leaders often fail to recognize the resources at their disposal. They often compare themselves to secular community leaders and see only the ways that pastors are disadvantaged. Bank presidents and small business owners, for example, have access to a range of options not open to churches. And a government official or a manager in some national corporation can draw on a host of resources that congregations can only dream about. We know that businesses can fire an unproductive worker or advertise for just the right person to fill a position; they don't have to rely solely on the volunteers that happen to show up at their congregations. Corporations can throw money at a problem and governments can enact laws to make people do what the politicians think is best. But churches cannot enact their wishes; they can only encourage, exhort, and entice. When compared with secular leaders it is clear that there are resources that Christian leaders often lack, resources such as money, buildings, votes, and prestige.

All that may or may not be true, but it is beside the point because of one fact. Congregational ministers enjoy one tremendous advantage that leaders of other organizations do not have. In no other organization is there a custom that says for twenty minutes each week the assembled organization must sit quietly while the leader of the organization talks about whatever the leader thinks is important. Bank presidents might gather employees for a two-minute pep talk. Corporations may send out routinely disregarded memos. And politicians may give poorly attended speeches. But none of them have their words standing as the focal point of the organization's central event.[1] The primary responsibility of most Protestant ministers is to be a theological interpreter. In other words, pastors make spiritual meaning. And that provides them with a huge organizational advantage.[2]

It is important, before we get too far into this analysis, to emphasize the theological nature of this interpretation. The reason that pastors have a different organizational role as compared to, say, bank presidents is that pastors bear a different responsibility—a theological responsibility. In many denominations, there is a tradition to ask, "Does anyone have a word from the Lord?" A sermon must be more than the musings of a thoughtful social commentator, and it must be more than a subtle attempt to maneuver people. It is first and foremost a word from the Lord. It is a matter of vocation. A minister is called to be the person who speaks God's word into a situation. I emphasize this primary responsibility because the ensuing discussion is going to emphasize theological interpretation as a tool for Christian leadership. But please do not misunderstand the larger point. We do the interpretation because that is our calling from God. That means that any discussion of leadership as interpretation must conform to the standards and responsibilities of that calling.[3]

A by-product of this calling is that ministers enjoy an organizational advantage that is unique. They get to speak each week. This is advantageous for a number of reasons. First, it gives preachers the venue to create a framework for interpretation. Often it takes time to introduce new ideas and to allow people to come to terms with new ways of seeing the world.[4] My philosophy on preaching is that it is rare for any one particular sermon to change someone dramatically, but if you give a preacher fifty-two weeks year after year, then he or she has time to transform a people. This is the homiletic analog to the oft-repeated statement that "we tend to overestimate what can be done in a year and underestimate what can be done in a decade." It takes time to build changes.[5] It takes time because a leader has to change the categories that people use to interpret their world. We learned from Ann Swidler that people are not going to easily change the stories they tell themselves to make sense of their worlds. So we have to

> Change the categories that people use to interpret their world.

get them to pay attention to new details and help them to cultivate different expectations. This will become clearer as part 2 unfolds. But the important point for now is that the only way to build new interpretative frameworks is to have regular opportunities for speech. And that opportunity comes naturally to pastors because each one has a calling to proclaim a word from the Lord.

The second reason that the preaching office is an organizational advantage for pastors is that it sets up ministers as theological interpreters in other congregational contexts as well. This means that in meetings, for example, people expect Christian leaders to provide a theological interpretation. That is why Rev. Charlotte Robinson's preference for Herb over Darien as Almond Springs' choir director carried so much weight. She made a theological argument when she said that Darien did not understand the sacraments. And people deferred to her judgment because providing a theological perspective is part of her role as pastor.

Indeed, the expectation that Christian leaders provide theological interpretation is so strong that it carries over to those who do not preach regularly. Associate ministers, for example, do not preach frequently. They are responsible instead for ministries such as visitation, education, children, and youth ministry. But the interpretive office extends to those ministries as well. Pastoral visitation is often about helping people to see their own situations in light of God's enveloping love. Children's ministry is likewise about providing the basic building blocks of a Christian perspective on the world. And youth ministry provides a context for teens to use Christian categories to make sense of adolescence. In each situation, the ordained Christian leader is the one who provides a framework for spiritual interpretation.

This, of course, extends naturally to those who lead without being ordained. It is deceptively easy to pretend that the work of the church divides into the holy and the profane—with ministers doing the holy work while laypeople do the profane. That would require, however, a fundamental misunderstanding of how God chooses to work in the world. The whole work of the church is the responsibility of the whole people of God. In other words, all Christian leaders—lay and clergy alike—bear a responsibility to provide theological interpretation for God's people. The "Old Man Rivers" episode that we discussed in part 1 provides a good example. It is Doc Davis who brings Gary Rivers to meet with Rev. Robinson. Charlotte may be the one who uses her pastoral office to tell Gary that God wants to forgive him and that he can one day be part of the very church that has rejected him. But something crucial happened before Gary walked into Charlotte's office. Doc told Gary two things. He told him that Charlotte can be trusted, as Gary reports, "even though you're a woman and all." And he told Gary that he should be baptized because, as Gary says, "it's part of that new creation thing." The pastor's role is simply to confirm what Doc has already told Gary. When Doc set Gary's experience in a theological context, he changed the very meaning of Gary's experience. And, in that moment, Doc was exercising his role as a Christian leader. The most significant pastoral care, in this and in so many situations, came from the layperson and not the pastor. Theological interpretation does not belong solely to the person who preaches.

The common theme is that Christian leaders make spiritual meaning. But that leads to the question of *how* Christian leaders make spiritual meaning. That is the burden of part 2 of the book: to describe the ways that this meaning-making leadership happens. In short, meaning-making leaders give people the vocabulary and theological categories to imagine a different way to interpret the world and to construct a new course of action that flows from that interpretation. The building blocks for this perspective on the world are what we will call "cultural resources." Part 2 thus will:

> Meaning-making leaders give people the vocabulary and theological categories to imagine a different way to interpret the world.

1. Explain what cultural resources are and give examples of how they are used in leadership.
2. Show how these cultural resources are bundled together to form subcultures.
3. Describe how meaning-making leaders shape meaning usng cultural resources.

These cultural resources then become the building blocks that pastors use to lead by making meaning.

Meaning-making Leaders Use Cultural Resources

We have already noted that secular leaders have access to some resources that Christian leaders often lack. They have access to money, buildings, workers, and votes. These are what we can call "structural resources." We should distinguish them from "cultural resources." They are called "'structural' resources" because they are connected to what sociologists call social structure.[6] The complement of social structure is culture.[7] Cultural resources differ from structural resources in that cultural resources must be interpreted in order to

> Structural resources (like money and laws) have the power to compel, while cultural resources have the power to persuade.

have power. At the end of the day, a politician can count votes, a businesswoman can add up dollars, and anyone can touch a building. But there is no way to total up ideas, values, or purposes. They exist in a person's mind and cannot be tallied on a sheet of paper. Because cultural resources cannot be unambiguously accumulated they are more ethereal than structural resources. They also retain a different kind of power. Cultural resources have a persuasive power because they can change a person's mind. Structural resources (like money and votes) can offer an enticement to act as if one's mind has changed, but their power to persuade will always be secondary to the power of ideas, values, and purposes.[8] When someone seeks to "do the right thing" they appeal to cultural resources rather than structural ones. And that is why cultural resources have such power. Structural resources (like money and laws) have the power to compel, while cultural resources have the power to persuade.

There is an analogous argument to be made about structural authority and cultural authority.[9] Structural authority is delineated and unambiguous, while cultural authority is ascribed. When a police officer makes an arrest or writes a ticket, he or she is using structural authority. If a person does not obey that officer's authority, there are clear and onerous penalties (such as prison). Likewise, a supervisor maintains a structural authority over someone when his or her job description says that the person reports to that supervisor. Structural authority has clear demarcations that often include penalties for failure to recognize that authority. Cultural authority, on the other hand, is freely given rather than assigned; the person who recognizes the authority gives it. For example, in many cultures elderly people are honored with particular respect. No written law requires that younger people should revere them, but we all have heard the phrase, "Respect your elders." Cultural authority cannot be taken; it must be given.

The dispute between Charlotte Robinson and her first choir director, Jan Neuski, turned on just this distinction between cultural and structural sources of power and authority. Charlotte believed that her pastoral office gave her the power to construct the worship service (including the hymns) and the authority to supervise the choir director. Jan noted that these were cultural—and therefore ascribed—prerogatives. And she declined to recognize them. Jan thus ignored the hymns that were listed in the bulletin and announced new ones to the congregation. That is, she ignored the pastor's authority because the authority was not delineated anywhere in writing. Charlotte responded by trying to make the pastor's power and authority structural. She had the Personnel Committee draw up a job description that defined her supervisory authority over the choir director and delineated her power over the worship service. Both Charlotte and Jan knew that the pastor could not really control the choir director so long as the minister only had cultural power and authority. As soon as the Personnel Committee approved the job description, both parties knew that the pastor had won and the choir director had lost. The pastor now had all the structural power. So Jan resigned.

Charlotte may have won that battle, but it is not clear that she acted faithfully—to the extent that acting faithfully demands that one maintain a consistency between the gospel we preach and the action we take. I would argue that in this situation, the pastor might have been more interested in getting her way than in treating Jan with respect. At some point, Charlotte subconsciously declared war on Jan and allowed herself to suspend the normal rules for faithful action. Thus we have to ask if there is another way to lead. Is there a way to draw on the lessons about meaning making from part 1 in order to see leadership in a new light?

> What Christian leaders lack in structural resources they make up for in cultural resources.

Charlotte believed that her problem was a lack of structural resources, so she got some new rules passed that gave her those resources. But I am going to argue that structural resources are not the most important resources for meaning-making leaders. I am going to argue that what Christian leaders lack in structural resources they make up for in cultural resources.

Relying on cultural resources allows a different leadership model than the one built around structural resources. Business leaders strive to control their worlds by gathering monetary resources, accumulating votes, and writing regulations.[10] Their power is coercive, and their authority restrictive.[11] Religious leaders rarely have access to this kind of structural authority.[12] They cannot enforce their will, nor should they wish to. Instead, religious leaders rely on rhetorical authority, the power to convince and persuade— but not to coerce. They cannot make people obey them, but they can inspire people to follow them. That's what I mean when I say that what pastors lack in structural resources they make up for with cultural resources.[13]

James Hopewell provides an example of leadership that builds on cultural resources. He adopted what he called a permissive leadership style as an Episcopal priest. He described himself as "unaggressive and nonauthoritative." "By sitting sympathetically through a year's worth of meetings, conflicts, services, and conversations," he reported, "I sought to determine what [the parish's] participants were saying to each other, what meanings they were sharing, what drama they as actors were together unfolding." He found "a fascinating tapestry woven with distinctive values and outlooks and behaviors." This led him to conclude that, "a congregation is held together by much more than creeds, governing structures, and programs. At a deeper level, it is implicated in the symbols and signals of the world, gathering and grounding them in the congregation's own idiom." By idiom Hopewell means, "a wondrously complex language, largely built of written and spoken words and phrases, but also including matter as tangible as doughnuts and mute as handshakes and pouts."[14] This wondrously complex language of symbols and signals is built from what we are calling here cultural resources.

I refer to cultural resources as resources because they are the building blocks that leaders use to construct their interpretations of the world.[15] Each captures a different sense of what religion means and each defines a different element of what is most meaningful about the religious group's communal understanding of itself. I have identified six such cultural resources: community, beliefs, values, purposes, narrative, and practices (see Table 1).[16] The culture of each congregation or religious organization (and of each subgroup therein) tends to have within it some combination of these resources.[17]

Table 1. Leading with Cultural Resources: The Building Blocks of Shared Vision

To Understand:	Look at:	Ask:	Definitions of Religion	Evangelicals	Mainline Protestants
COMMUNITY	Boundaries & Connections	What holds the group together? What separates insiders from outsiders?	Religion as Culture (Cultural Anthropology)	Theology	Social Action
IDEOLOGY (Theology)	Beliefs	What ideas guide the group's actions?	Religion as Theological Belief	Substitutionary Atonement Biblical Authority	Individual Rights Multiculturalism
NORMS	Values	What characteristics does the group hope to embody?	Religion as Morality	"Family Values" Holiness Unity	Tolerance Mercy Freedom
GOALS	Purpose	What results does the group hope to achieve?	Religion as Activism	Evangelization Righteousness	Justice Peace
NARRATIVE & RITUAL	Dream/Vision	Is there a unifying theme/story that holds these together?	Religion as Ritual Religion as Journey Religion as Conversion	Conversion Narratives "Once I was lost, now I am found."	"Faith Journey" "We are all on a journey of faith."
PRACTICES	Practices	What tradition-bearing activities characterize the group?	Religion as Practices	"Quiet Time" Tithing	Peacemaking

1. Community as a cultural resource

The first cultural resource that meaning-making leaders use is *community*. Another name for it might be "insiderness." It refers to what holds the group together. To find it, look at the boundaries that separate insiders from outsiders and at the connections that bind the community together. Women's groups call this sisterhood. Ethnic groups can refer to their ethnicity. Labor unions rally around class loyalty. And religious groups identify themselves by their faith. That is what happens, for example, when this book distinguishes Christian leadership from secular forms of leading. But Christianity is large enough to get parsed into smaller components. Denominational identity is thus another common marker of community. When people say, "we Methodists . . . " or they talk about "the Lutheran way of doing things . . . " they are referring to how "our" community is different from others.[18]

Locale is another common marker. Some congregations have members who tend to live in the same area. For example, the Woodside Lutheran Church (where we met our teenage friend Mindy) is distinguished from the Riverside Lutheran Church because the eastern portion of the town was once near the woods and the western portion of the town was near the river. The fact that the woods are now tract homes does not change the fact that the area is still called Woodside. And the church tends to draw most of its members from the immediate neighborhood. The sociologist Nancy Ammerman calls such location-based churches "parish congregations" because what binds their members together is the location of their homes. Such churches describe themselves as having a spiritual responsibility for the people who live in their area, whether or not the people who live there actually attend the church.[19] Almond Springs Presbyterian Church fits this description.

Ammerman contrasts the parish congregation with what she calls a "niche congregation." In a niche congregation, members come from diverse locales but they share some demographic quality—that is, the congregation fills a demographic niche. People drive from many miles, for example, to attend the church where I belong. Some of the members, it is true, come from the local area. But those who do drive a ways tend to share a number of characteristics. They tend, for example, to be well educated and often are associated with one of the colleges in the area. In contrast to the professor-rich congregation I presently attend, the church where I grew up had (and still has) a wealth of doctors, nurses, and other medical professionals. And each of these churches shared an upper-middle-class, white outlook on the world. I love my congregation. But a visitor who did not much like being in school when they were a child is going to be uncomfortable in, say, the adult Sunday school class that is so important to our congregation. It is run almost like a seminary class, with a dual emphasis on learning and faithfulness. That's what most of the people who attend the class like most about it. But it is also the thing that would likely alienate others who did not share this congregation's nerdy love for learning. The congregation fills a niche. It appeals to a specific slice of the world. It's not as if other folks are discouraged from attending. But it is likely that people who do not happen to fall into this niche would feel more at home in a different congregation.

There are those who would like to make value judgments about the ethics of niche congregations and, indeed, all attempts at making insiders. Some believe, as a matter of ecclesiology, that no congregation should do anything to make someone feel unwelcome. And the very language of insider and of community, so the argument goes, is an affront to the God who welcomes all peoples regardless of station. I would disagree with this logic. The very acts of hospitality that some folks will find welcoming will seem off-putting and inhospitable to other people. A congregation that is particularly welcoming to any one segment of the population does so by being dissimilar to another segment of the population. A congregation that reaches out to GenXers, for example, will necessarily feel foreign to someone from a traditional congregation.[20] And, in my congregation, there are many people who feel that the emphasis on theological rigor signals to them that a person can bring their whole self—including their mind—into the worship of God. Others might take a different attitude and call it elitist.

Even the congregations that work hard to "be all things to all people," to use the Apostle Paul's phrase, necessarily draw boundaries. There are congregations, for example, that offer Starbucks coffee to parishioners as they enter the worship service. I select this example because it is not particularly controversial at present. But once the example is clear, I trust that you will see that its significance would be magnified if I'd chosen a more contentious situation. These coffee-serving congregations see that gesture as an act of hospitality. Other congregations see it as a sacrilegious act that should never be allowed. (And, of course, there are many congregations that are less concerned about sacrilege than about stains on the carpet.) But as soon as a congregation decides whether or not to serve coffee before the service, they have set up a boundary—whether they intend to or not. Some people will agree with them. Some may disagree. The measure of hospitality is not about whether a congregation has boundaries, but instead about the extent to which those outside their boundaries are welcomed into the congregation's midst.[21]

How then can this notion of "community" become a cultural resource that enables a meaning-making leadership? It provides, as does each cultural resource, a basis for mobilizing a congregation. For example, put yourself in the position of Reverend Charlotte Robinson of Almond Springs Presbyterian Church. By the spring of her first year in town, she began to have a wonderful problem. The church needed more Sunday school teachers for elementary school children. The church had never really had much of a Sunday school. Kids were not divided into classes; kindergarteners through sixth-graders were in the same room. One dedicated stalwart (Hazel Moore) took two Sundays a month. She taught a lesson and worked out a craft for the kids to do, often enlisting the older kids to help the younger ones. When Hazel was not the teacher, the volunteers were often more like babysitters than teachers in that they rarely followed a lesson plan. This arrangement worked before Charlotte came because there were so few kids in the Sunday school. In her first nine months, however, the number of children had more than tripled, overwhelming what the pastor called "the one-room-schoolhouse approach to Sunday school." Upon meeting with the newly reconstituted Education Committee, it was determined that the pastor should write a letter to the congregation explaining the situation and asking for more teachers.

One way for Rev. Robinson to seek teachers would be to rely on "community" cultural resources that emphasize insiderness. She could highlight the congregation's identity as Presbyterians, a denomination that has a long history of cherishing education. She could highlight the congregation's place in the town, contrasting her congregation to, say, the Roman Catholic or Assemblies of God churches in Almond Springs. She could contrast the Almond Springs church with other Presbyterian congregations such as her former church in San Jose. Or, she could talk about Christians, say, as a beleaguered minority soldiering on in the face of the harsh secular world.[22]

Notice, however, how each of these strategies seems a bit parochial. This is a common problem when a leader appeals to only one cultural resource without reference to other cultural resources. It can often appear stark or jarring. Indeed, in this particular case, appealing to communal identity without the other cultural resources feels self-serving. It seems a bit like, for example, Presbyterians have a corner on education or that the pastor thinks her congregation is better than, say, the Roman Catholic parish. Thus, after I define each of the cultural resources, I will show how to bind them together into a whole that is greater than the sum of its parts.

2. Beliefs as a cultural resource

The second cultural resource available to a Christian leader is a people's *beliefs*. In this context, beliefs refer to the ideas that are central to a group of people's self-understanding and to the theology that guides their actions. Many Christians make theology tantamount to Christianity itself. They take for granted that subscription to particular theological tenets is the boundary line between sacred and profane—indeed, between Christian and non-Christian. Table 1 shows, for example, one way of looking at how Evangelicals and Mainline Protestants[23] differ in their beliefs.[24] Each group has ideas that form the core of its communal identity. But each builds on different theological commitments. This disparity is one of the primary reasons that the two groups often talk past each other. Evangelicals emphasize substitutionary atonement and biblical authority, just as the Mainline emphasizes individual rights and multiculturalism. Members of an Evangelical congregation do not have to defend substitutionary atonement; they simply equate "accepting Jesus as your Lord and Savior" with being a Christian. Likewise, Mainline congregations do not explain why they emphasize rights; they take for granted that governments should, in the words of Proverbs. "Speak up for those who cannot speak for themselves, for the rights of all who are destitute. Speak up and judge fairly; defend the rights of the poor and needy" (31:8-9 NIV). Beliefs form the core of most congregations' self-perception.

Theology is, of course, central to a leader's attempts to help a people make spiritual meaning. Christian leaders create a theological framework for understanding situations in the world. In Almond Springs, for example, there was an enormous community debate over whether or not to build a housing development. The minister, Charlotte Robinson, understood the controversy over the housing development in theological terms. On the one hand, she saw that a parishioner named Ansel Richards opposed the development because he believed that one of the primary human responsibilities is the stewardship of the earth. This stewardship has a long theological tradition rooted in the mandate that God gave Adam in the garden of Eden to "have dominion" over the earth. Christians have for generations seen this mandate as more than a license to exploit the earth's resources. They have also seen it, in the language of one Presbyterian creed, as a prohibition against the sinful tendency to "exploit neighbor and nature."[25] On the other hand, the pastor saw that a second parishioner, named Louis Walsh, was fueled by a motivation to build the housing development that emanated from a deep sense of Christian responsibility as well. He believed that the rural town was dying—"becoming hollow" were his words—because so many people were moving away and that the poor were always the first to suffer as the result of such economic trials. Another congregant, Doc Davis, framed the question as a health issue. He believed that there needed to be a minimal level of economic viability in order for people to be able to afford adequate health care. Without an economic substructure, Doc believed that the poor would suffer. In short, Charlotte frames her dilemma theologically by saying that each side represents an attempt to be faithful to a spiritual responsibility. Doc and Louis want to care for the poor, while Ansel wants to care for the environment.

At first this conflict of theological commitments put Rev. Robinson on the sidelines of the public debate. She was not sure if she should step in to the controversy. Nor was she sure how she could step in even if she was so inclined. Charlotte eventually realized that the best way to mediate the theological controversy was to point to the spiritual issues that lay beneath the surface—the ones that no one was talking about. She decided that the best way to address these concerns was to return to the congregation's mission statement because she saw a common spiritual denominator that characterized both sides of the debate. "Fear. Anxiety about the future," Charlotte told Laura Webber at one point, "these are spiritual categories. How can I say that our church's mission is to proclaim, 'God's Hope for Our Future,' if I am going to remain on the sidelines when the community is dealing with its fear?"[26] So she devoted the weeks leading up to the great town debate to preaching about fear.

Notice what happened here, something that is absolutely essential to the role of a spiritual leader as a meaning maker. She decided that the key issue for the town was neither economics nor the environment. She decided that the key question was fear. "Can God be trusted to provide a hopeful future?" she asked her congregation. She framed the issue that way because, if God could not be trusted, then it did not really matter whether the town pursued prosperity or preserved the environment. Rev. Charlotte Robinson provided spiritual leadership because she pointed to the deeper theological questions behind the issues that her town was debating. She named aloud the questions that kept people awake at night. That is theological leadership.

Beliefs are particularly powerful cultural resources because they are often taken for granted. One of the reasons that Christians often talk past each other when discussing controversial issues is that people often have different definitions for the same theological ideas. Evangelicals and Mainline Protestants, for example, each believe that one of the central Christian practices is "witness." They each see it as central to the mission of the church. However, the two factions define witness very differently and consequently have difficulty agreeing on how to do cooperative mission. When Evangelicals talk about "witnessing," they have in mind an evangelistic encounter such as when Jose tells Mary about an experience of soul-redeeming release that came when he first confessed his sin to God and invited Jesus to forgive that sin. There is an ideological aspect built into the Evangelical notion of witness in that a new convert needs to understand a modicum of theology in order to believe the truth of the gospel. Mainline Protestants, on the other hand, think of witness as a public demonstration of God's longing for justice in the world. Taking a principled public stand on an issue or participating in a protest march would be an act of witness, as would writing a letter to the editor or boycotting an oppressive company. The ideology or belief built into the Mainline Protestant notion of witness involves the specific way that the biblical concept of justice is translated into contemporary life. For example, individual rights are usually quite important to Mainline belief. So the logic of the Mainline says that, because the church should oppose attempts to restrict individual rights, any public action that opposes such attempts is thus an act of Christian witness. Evangelicals and Mainline Protestants share a commitment to witness. They disagree, however, over what exactly it means to witness.

Thus beliefs (or ideology) [27] can divide a people. But beliefs can also be a way to unite a people. Each week preachers appeal to theology as they attempt to motivate people. Evangelical preachers tell their congregations of God's love and ask their congregants to engage that week in evangelism. By the same token, Mainline preachers use the language of the prophets to tell their congregations about how God's love demands justice in the world. They use that language to ask their congregants to open doors for people who are not like themselves. Indeed, one of the most common Christian sermons is a theological sermon with a section at the end designed to use that theology to motivate people to act in the world. Beliefs can be a powerful cultural resource.[28]

What, then, would such theological leadership look like when dealing with the example of recruiting new Sunday school teachers? There are at least two ways that the pastor could go. She could either frame the theological calling of teachers or she could emphasize the importance of teachers in inculcating theology to children. First, she could frame the teaching office theologically.[29] She might write something like this, "God grants to each Christian gifts that build up the whole body of Christ. Some, like me, are indeed called to be ministers. But each person in this congregation has gifts from God. Many of you would be gifted teachers, if you would only give yourself the chance to discover that gift. This is the time to explore that teaching gift. We all rejoice that we have so many new kids in our Sunday school. Where once one or two teachers were needed, now we need at least eight each week. Many of you have the gifts to teach our children. Now is the time to exercise that giftedness." Such a statement frames teaching as a calling from God. And it makes it that much harder for someone to think of Sunday school as glorified babysitting. The prob-lem, of course, with casting teaching as a calling from God is that many people would be intimidated. Those who do not fully understand that God calls each person could easily see this as a message for Christians who are more mature than they are. One way to deal with that fear would be to pair the first kind of theological appeal with a second one.

The second kind of theological appeal for teachers would talk about the importance of inculcating children with the rudiments of belief. The pastor might write something like this, "We have a tremendous privilege at Almond Springs Church. Each week more and more parents ask us to educate their children in the faith of Jesus Christ. The only way to do that is to add classes. And we need teachers for those classes. No one needs to be a pillar of the faith to teach our kids. Nor do they need to be able to quote from Calvin's *Institutes* (you don't even have to know who John Calvin was). But you do need to be able to tell children what you do know. Our kids need people to introduce them to the faith. They need someone to tell them, at Christmas, about why God sent the baby Jesus to be born to peasant Jews. And they need someone to tell them, at Easter, why Jesus chose to die so that we might have life. That's what Sunday school teachers do. They introduce children to the stories that will animate kids' faith for the rest of their lives. Do you want to help form a child's faith?" Such an appeal emphasizes what beliefs do and why they matter. Beliefs are the second cultural resource.

3. Values as a cultural resource

The third cultural resource available to the meaning-making leader is *values*. Another name for values is norms. To locate what values matter most in a community, ask what characteristics a people hope to embody. When we say that Christians should be honest and kind, for example, we are describing values that we hope Christians will embody.

When Evangelicals talk about values, they emphasize personal holiness and what are often called "family values." Mainline Protestants, on the other hand, emphasize values such as tolerance, mercy, and freedom. As with theology, it is easy to see why these two groups so often talk past each other. They hope to embody and to instill a very different set of values in their congregations. This is not to say, for example, that an Evangelical congregation would be opposed to mercy or tolerance—nor would a Mainline congregation be opposed to personal holiness. The crux comes when values are in conflict with one another. Many of the ecclesiastical controversies of our day come down to a matter of emphasis. Which is more important: the unity of the whole or freedom for the individual? Evangelicals tend toward normative values that are imposed on all members of the community for the sake of holiness, purity, and unity. Evangelicals will choose purity even at the cost of freedom. Mainline Protestants tend to make the opposite choice. They tend to value tolerance and freedom so highly that they are willing sacrifice unity in order to preserve the right of individuals to make their own judgments before God.[30] Either way, values are clearly very important to American Christians.

This, of course, allows leaders to make meaning by pointing to values. Congregations often act because of the values that they hold most dear. For example, a significant motivation for congregational youth work is to inculcate values. Churches see themselves as standing over against the values that are expressed in the larger culture, especially the media. The stereotype for this may be the sexual norms that churches proclaim. And these are indeed important. But I have in mind something even more basic. One of the most common topics of conversation for church youth groups revolves around acceptance, kindness, and compassion. Youth leaders regularly talk about how to treat other people. That is where we get the discussions of cliques and conversations about in-crowds and out-crowds. Churches regularly spend a great deal of their youth-directed energy inculcating values.

Pastors sometimes end up teaching about values even when they have other issues on their minds—as Rev. Charlotte Robinson learned. Charlotte often retreated to a cabin by a lake to write her sermon. The cabin belonged to Stuart Dolman, the congregation's treasurer. One day in early fall, she encounterd Stuart's wife Brandi, a woman in a particularly interesting moral state. Brandi had, for most of her adult life, not followed the norms that one usually associates with Christianity. This is most obviously manifest in multiple extramarital affairs. But her moral state is particularly interesting because she was, in her fifties, rethinking her values. In something akin to an inverse midlife crisis, she visited her husband's pastor to begin to make moral sense of her life. What's important here, for our discussion of cultural resources, is that Brandi could not initially separate Christian values from Christianity itself. She saw living a moral life as the very definition of being a Christian. This view is fairly common among people who know little about Christianity. And it can be both a hindrance and a help to a pastor's work. Brandi immaturely tried to bait Charlotte when they first met by shocking her with profanity and alcohol. When the pastor did not immediately condemn the woman, an opening for trust appeared that allowed Brandi, over time, to explore the questions that pained her. But Brandi's questions went beyond values, even if she herself did not know it. What's interesting is the way that Charlotte, as Brandi's pastor, used the moral conversations as an entrance into deeper discussions about the state of Brandi's soul. In other words, Brandi came to Charlotte with moral questions about values, but Charlotte challenged her to see that she was also asking spiritual questions as well.

There are other ways that leaders use moral resources in Almond Springs. One of the most interesting examples involves Hazel Moore's discussion with Ansel Richards about the controversial housing development. It is interesting because one way that moral logic is often used as a resource (albeit incorrectly) is to demonize one's opponents. Ansel presents himself to Hazel, the town librarian, as a searcher for the truth. He comes to the library to do research about the housing development. But Ansel finds Hazel's reaction disconcerting, not because of the ideas she presents to him, but because of the moral fiber that she exemplifies. He wants to demonize everyone who disagrees with him. Yet she helps him find articles that might allow Ansel to argue against Hazel's new husband, Doc Davis. Her willingness to help him begins to defeat his generalization that the opposition is morally suspect. She exhibits personal qualities that appeal to Ansel. This allows him to explore with her his own position on the development. He finds that she thinks he is wrong and the way that she has chosen to express her disagreement disarms him enough to re-examine his own position. There was something in Hazel's character that allowed Ansel to hear things that, up until that point, he had been closed off from hearing. The values or characteristics that Hazel embodied were the key to enabling Ansel's newfound openness.

As we turn to Charlotte Robinson's recruitment of Sunday school teachers, there are once again at least a couple of ways that the pastor could appeal to values in writing her letter to the congregation. She could select a value such as duty to be at the center of her appeal, or she could describe what the absence of values would do to children. First we'll look at how she might focus on a value like duty or faithfulness. Most Christians (indeed most Americans) value "pulling your own weight." They believe that every person has certain responsibilities that he or she has a duty to perform. So Charlotte might write something like this, "Every privilege comes with responsibility. We at Almond Springs Church are fortunate to be experiencing a season of God's blessing. In the last year, the number of children at our church has tripled. We rejoice that God has brought them into our midst. But that blessing brings a responsibility. We have a duty to educate these children in the ways of the Lord. So I am writing to ask each of you to do right by our children. Volunteer to be a Sunday school teacher. God has blessed our congregation with these precious young souls. Will you respond to the responsibility that comes with that blessing?" Since duty is a value that resonates within Rev. Robinson's church, she could use that value as a resource in recruiting teachers.

There are other ways that Charlotte could appeal to values. Just as she talked in the previous section about the need to form basic beliefs in children, so she could also describe Sunday school as a place that instills values. She might write something like, "Children entering our fractured world have very few places where they can learn the values at the heart of the Christian faith, values embodied in commandments such as 'honor thy mother and father' and 'love thy neighbor as thyself.' Video games teach kids to destroy aliens and music videos teach them to indulge their passions. But where will they learn about the compassion of the Good Samaritan and the self-sacrificing love of the God who sent Jesus to die that we might have life? They can learn those values in Sunday school. And we at Almond Springs Church have a wonderful opportunity. The number of kids at our church has tripled in the last few months. And now we need Sunday school teachers, lots of them. Will you be the one to tell our children about the forgiving love that welcomes the prodigal home? Or do you think kids should learn their values from video games and TV? Come help us build our children." I recognize that such a forthright appeal to values would feel heavy-handed in some congregations. I also know that it would fit within the culture of other congregations. Either way, it illustrates the way that a leader might appeal to values as a motivation for people to become Sunday school teachers.

4. Goals and purposes as cultural resources

The fourth cultural resource available to meaning-making leaders revolves around *goals and purposes*. Every congregation or religious organization has a reason for being, a goal whose pursuit justifies the very existence of the organization. Locating this purpose in religious nonprofits is usually quite easy. The reason a soup kitchen exists is to provide meals to the poor. The purpose of a Christian counseling center is to provide psychological aid from a Christian perspective. But asking about the purpose of a congregation is more difficult. Different theological traditions each have their own ecclesiological answers for why the church exists. This is, however, a good time to point back to Chris Argyris's distinction between the ideas we espouse and the actions that we actually embody. The theological answer to the what's-the-purpose-of-a-congregation question belongs in the discussion of beliefs as a cultural resource. It is indeed an important resource. But that's not what I am talking about here. There also exists within each congregation a set of actions that congregants believe are at the heart of what it means to be the church. Indeed, some Christians see activism as being the very definition of faith. They point to the New Testament book of James that says, "Faith without works is dead." Those congregations want to be judged not by the beliefs that they espouse but by the actions they take.[31]

Congregations regularly experience disagreements and controversies about how to understand the relationship of faith and action. For the last few pages, we have used the divergent approaches of Evangelicals and Mainline Protestants to show how to understand cultural resources. This works as well with purposes. Evangelicals cherish one set of goals for the church, while the Mainline takes for granted that the church has a different purpose. Evangelicals believe that the purpose of the church is to save souls, and they emphasize evangelism as the primary means to that end. Mainline Protestants believe that the purpose of the church is to save society, and they pursue justice and peace as the primary means to that end. Notice that each tradition takes for granted its mandate, which is called "witness" in each tradition. Evangelicals do not try to defend evangelism as a goal; they simply pursue it by teaching congregants to witness to their neighbors. Likewise, the Mainline does not defend peace-making as a goal; they simply pursue it by teaching congregants how to witness for peace in society.

Our discussion of goals as a cultural resource points to another tension built into Christianity. It is the inherent tension between internally focused purposes and externally oriented ones. For example, many Christians would argue that congregations exist for the worship of God. And they would be right. This is why so many pastors like to quote the opening of the Westminster Catechism, which says that "the chief end of man is to glorify God and enjoy Him forever." A church that does not worship makes as little sense as scuba gear in the Sahara. Once the church has lost this reason for being, it might as well be a museum piece. But worship is not the only reason a church exists. We are, like Abraham, "blessed to be a blessing." Churches are called into the world to preach good news to the lost and release to the captives. So alongside the internally directed purpose of worship,[32] each congregation must have ministries that take its people beyond its walls. Thus each congregation has externally-focused purposes that exist alongside the internally directed ones. This becomes important because these two types of purposes often compete against one another within a given congregation. Usually this happens when one group of parishioners gravitates toward some external ministry like a soup kitchen, while the majority of a congregation remains focused on internal activities like choir and Sunday school. The soup kitchen folks often "can't understand why more people aren't really committed to the purpose of the church, which is to serve the poor"—even as some overtaxed mother of three wonders what more she can do than teach third graders, decorate the bulletin boards in the narthex, drive the church van for youth events, and take communion to shut-ins on Sunday afternoons. The very meaning of the word "committed" depends on whether one talks about internally or externally focused purposes. And these competing purposes create for many congregants a sense that "we" (i.e., "people who see things the way I do") are the only ones who are really committed.

What is a meaning-maker leader to do when such a competition over purposes exists? A leader's responsibility is to provide a theological framework that allows people to make new sense of their situation. The first step in such a situation is simply to name the terrain—to say aloud, in multiple contexts, that the church has multiple purposes and that the people of God have both internal responsibilities and external ones. There are a host of biblical images that might help such a leader. The "body of Christ" image comes most quickly to mind because its purpose is to warn God's people not to think that any one ministry or Christian is more important than the others.

This leads us, quite naturally, back to Rev. Charlotte Robinson's need to recruit Sunday school teachers. But in this case, we might add the restriction that she needs to do her recruiting in such a way that it does not detract from the externally directed ministries of the church. Thus she might write something like this, "Someone once said that 'the church exists for mission as a flame exists for burning.' What that means is that the reason Christ's church exists is to do the work of ministry in the world. Some of these ministries take place outside the church's walls, even as other ministries take place within its space. For example, Dorcas and Lazarus Pha are living testimony to the refugee resettlement work that this church has done in order to serve people beyond our shores. And the renewed work of the Outreach Committee is bearing wonderful fruit. We have had more than a dozen new families come into the church in the last few months. But that external work brings internal responsibilities as well. The Sunday school has now tripled in size. So we need teachers who will work with these beautiful young people. You all have no doubt heard that the church is the body of Christ and that each person within Christ's church is vital to that body. Some hands reach out and bring new families into our midst. Other hands scoop up those new children that come and teach them Christ's love. Where will you fit into Christ's body? The Spirit that burned at Pentecost is bringing light and hope to Almond Springs. That is why we exist. Come and bring your hands to bear God's love to the children of our Sunday school." Christian leaders can appeal to purposes as they make meaning.

5. Narrative and ritual as cultural resources

The fifth cultural resource available to meaning-making leaders revolves around *narrative and ritual*.[33] Within every community of faith there are stories or rituals that weave together the beliefs, values, and purposes of a people. There are stories that the group always seems to tell. And these are the heroes, or people whom the group lifts up as shining examples for all to see. This dependence on narrative is nothing new for God's people. Two stories permeated the life of the Hebrews: the call of

Abraham and the Exodus from Egypt. Throughout the Old Testament, God said (either directly or through the prophets), "I am the God of Abraham, Isaac, and Jacob." God's very identity among the people was tied to the stories of the patriarchs and the matriarchs. Indeed, the call of Abraham and Sarah (in Genesis 12 and 15) is indistinguishable from the call to the people of Israel. The covenant that God made with Abraham became the covenant that covered all of Abraham's heirs. That's why the story of Abraham became the founding narrative that gave God's people their very identity.[34] So the identity of God and the identity of God's people sprang forth from the stories of Abraham and Sarah, Isaac and Rebekah, and Jacob and his family. Likewise, the Exodus from Egypt served as a paradigm for the way that God remained faithful to God's faithless people. The long-suffering love of God that endures became perhaps the defining characteristic of God for the prophets. God renewed the covenant with Moses and for generations to come said to the people, "I am the LORD your God who brought you out of Egypt." Throughout the troubled history of Israel, the prophets reminded the struggling people that the God who redeemed them from Egyptian bondage could rescue them still. Then they used the story to call the people to repentance. The story became a paradigm. It solidified the identity of the people and the place of the God who would not forsake them.

Narratives are central to the religious identity of any people. The psychologist Jerome Bruner has written that stories become "recipes for structuring experience itself."[35] And Nancy Ammerman likewise notes that "religious narratives [are] the building blocks of individual and collective religious identities."[36] We carry with us a collection of religious narratives (think "tool kit" or "repertoire"). We draw from a confluence of religious narratives to create a framework for explaining our place in the world.[37] Some of those religious narratives are *public narratives* (like the stories of the Bible or from Christian history) that are available to all Christians.[38] Some are *communal narratives* (such as the ones a congregation tells itself). And some are intensely *personal narratives* that are only available to the persons involved. When I was a child, my family became involved in what, at that time, was called "the charismatic renewal." It was a renewed interest in the Holy Spirit that focused on lively worship services and prayers for specific healing. This movement pointed to stories in the book of Acts that describe miraculous acts performed by the Holy Spirit, and the movement believed such acts were available to God's people even today. In other words, they reinvigorated a particular set of neglected stories in order to claim their religious identity. This shows how public and communal narratives come together. But what about personal narratives; how do they fit in? I was about eight or nine years old at the time that my family became a part of this charismatic movement. So I did not have much of a personal narrative to tell. I simply appropriated my parents' religious identity. But one day, something happened that illustrates how a communal narrative can become intensely personal.

One day, while in third or fourth grade, I fell off a sled and opened a gash in my scalp. My mother dutifully put me in the back of the car and drove to the doctor while a neighbor kid applied pressure to the wound. And she did what any good charismatic mother would do in such a situation. She prayed while she drove. And since I was in the backseat, she prayed out loud for all to hear—including the taken-aback neighbor boy. When we got to the doctor's office, an intern came into the room and began with the obligatory, "How are you doing?" At that moment, I did not feel much pain in spite of all the blood. So I said to her, "It doesn't hurt. My mom prayed for me." I had appropriated for myself the healing narratives described in the book of Acts. This, of course, was not good enough for an incredulous intern. I am told that she poked and prodded the wound trying to evoke a shout of pain from me. None came. I was content while she sewed up the wound. That's when the head wound story became for me a personal religious narrative. Throughout my youth, I would hearken back in my mind to the tale as a reminder that God had visited me personally.[39] It was such an intense event for me because the public narrative of divine healing and the communal narrative of the charismatic renewal intersected for me at that moment with my personal story. We can generalize, then, to say that specific situations and settings "activate" particular religious narratives that then shape the meaning we make of the situation and our own role in it.[40]

These narratives are important both for the substance of the tales they tell and for the structure they provide. A person in despair, pleading with God, can recall the story of Jesus in the garden on the night he was betrayed. The story provides an implicit way for a person to see himself as persecuted but not forsaken. And the words Jesus prayed provide a model for the person to use as he asks God to "take this cup from me." But narrative works at a deeper level as well. Anyone who has spent much time in an evangelical congregation can testify to the pervasive power of the conversion narrative. The narrative structure says that people become Christians by turning from a life of sin to embrace the good news of the gospel. The structure presumes a dramatic turn. And that narrative structure carries so much weight for defining what it means to be Christian that an evangelical youth often must contort her life experience in order to fit it into this narrative of conversion. I experienced the power of this narrative form when my religious identity was being formed. I was raised in a situation that one could compare to Saul of Tarsus, who was born a "Hebrew of Hebrews." I grew up in the faith so that my parents' prayers were answered and I never departed from that faith. But when I reached a certain age, it came time for me to be "converted." My Sunday school teacher wanted me to "become a Christian," which meant turning from the life I was living and embracing a Christian life. Or at least that was how it was explained to me. But I had already embraced the Christian life as best as a third grader knew how. The more appropriate thing, I know now, would have been for the church to provide me a forum to make a formal declaration of faith. But the narrative form is so strong among Evangelicals that my teachers would not consider me a Christian until I could say, "once I was lost, but now I am found." I had to fit into the story in order to fit into the faith. To be an evangelical Christian meant conforming myself to the evangelical Christian story.[41]

I may have outgrown that narrative structure and now know that conversion is probably not the best way to describe the way that I appropriated the faith that my parents handed down to me.[42] But I do believe that it is crucial for the church to continue telling the story of faith and providing its people with the models for constructing their own religious identities. There are some who believe that the church is diminished when we describe the history of God's caring revelation as mere storytelling. Those people compared the stories we Christians tell to the equations that engineers build and the explanations that scientists construct. And they say that mere stories lack the certainty to compete with science. I believe those people disregard the complexity of life, which can neither be reduced to equations nor explained with a structured certainty. Indeed, we need the flexibility that stories provide so that we can appropriate the faith anew with each generation.[43] As the sociologist Robert Wuthnow said, "The idea of

> We need the flexibility that stories provide so that we can appropriate the faith anew with each generation.

church as storyteller may seem to diminish its importance, but this function has utmost significance. The very likelihood of anyone in the future retaining the identity 'Christian' depends on it."[44] Religious identity has a narrative form.[45]

Because religious identity takes a narrative form, meaning-making leaders rely on stories to help people make sense of their worlds. We know, for example, that expectations shape how people interpret new situations. People often carry those expectations in story form. That is why the practical theologians Anderson and Foley refer to our stories as "the premise of experience." They go on to say that, "Our collective life experiences are interpreted through a personal narrative framework and shaped into the master story that, in turn, influences subsequent interpretations."[46] The story we are telling ourselves as we interpret a situation constructs our expectations—expectations that lead us to look for certain cues and to ignore others.

The rituals we enact complement the stories we tell. "We are a people who not only narrate meaning-laden stories with our lips," according to Anderson and Foley, "but who also perform them with our bodies." This leads them to conclude, "For human beings, narrative and ritual are symbiotic."[47] We have to be careful here about the implications of the term *ritual*. For some it conjures nothing more than stale images of medieval priests wearing self-important robes while reciting Latin phrases they do not understand. But every congregation has rituals. It could be the way that the greeters shake hands with people on the way into the sanctuary, or the way the pastor shakes their hands as they leave. It could be the way that the ushers collect the offering during the service, or the way they seat people before it. Congregations have regularized activities that are all but invisible to insiders—and often opaque to outsiders. Rituals take on a narrative quality in that they become the familiar plot points that the congregation visits each week as it retells its story to itself.

The familiarity of the ritual can be a resource for reminding a congregation of its essential unity. For example, I recently heard an Episcopal priest describe the ironies of his congregation. He talked about how, on the one hand, his congregation is quite liberal in that it is known for taking progressive stances on social issues. Indeed, the congregation has a regional reputation as a bellwether of liberalism. Yet, according to the pastor, the congregation is deeply conservative on liturgical issues. Controversial social stands elicit rarely a peep from the congregation, but any change in the ritual creates an immediate wave of outraged letters.

Even moving liturgical furniture causes consternation. The pastor then drew a conclusion from this irony. He said that ritual stability enabled the congregation to venture into uncharted social territory. The congregation could take deep comfort in the ways that the liturgy united them, no matter how some of their fellow congregants might disagree on social questions.

This example could be a paradigm for one of the ways that cultural resources work. Stability on one level (say, with beliefs or values) allows a congregation to be innovative on another level (say, with purposes or goals). Remember Heifetz's axiom that we can only "fail people's expectations at a rate they can stand." Now we have one way to measure how much disruption people can stand. If a leader knows that she is going to have to do something controversial or disruptive, she can find another place to emphasize unity. This works especially well if the disruptive element proceeds from the unifying resource. For example, we discussed earlier how theological conservatives tend to take politically conservative stands on social issues like capital punishment and abortion. But we indicated in the notes that there was one exception. There is a group of Evangelicals who have articulated what they call a "completely pro-life" stance that opposes capital punishment for the same reasons that it opposes abortion.[48] They argue for ideological unity by taking the biblical passages on the sanctity of human life that Evangelicals associate with abortion and applying them to capital punishment. Thus they minimize the disruptive qualities of their new ethical argument by emphasizing the unifying qualities of their theological argument. In short, they use unity on beliefs as a resource for making a new argument about morality and ethics.

> Stability on one level (say, with beliefs or values) allows a congregation to be innovative on another level (say, with purposes or goals).

Narrative and ritual share another quality that helps meaning-making leaders. Any given ritual or narrative can make a range of different meanings.[49] This allows people to find meaning in the same story or ritual even if they interpret the story or the ritual in quite divergent ways. Let's look at an all too familiar example, the case when congregants say, "We've always done it that way." Say a particular congregation hosts its own little Christmas pageant each year. The script goes back many years and is attributed to a Sunday school superintendent who has long since passed away. She designed the pageant so that kids from each grade had specific roles (kindergarteners, for example, were sheep and second-graders were angels). One year it appeared that the leaders were going to change the script to update some of the more "quaint" passages (such as the one that emphasizes that the baby Jesus did not cry, which is a reference to "Away in a Manager" rather than a vestige from the Bible). There was an unexpected uproar among parents, even those who would normally have been in favor of the kinds of changes that the new script proposed. At first glance, this seems like a classic example of the frequently encountered "we've always done it that way" problem. Pastors are often amazed at the allergy some congregations have to change. But I would suggest that there is something deeper going on here. The pageant had been performed for so many years in a row that it became part of the ritual of Advent for that congregation. It had meaning apart from the script and the words on the page. If one were to investigate the reasons why it became controversial to change the pageant, one would find that there was not just one reason. Some would certainly fall into the we-don't-like-change category. But others would have more specific reasons. It seems that there were children who looked forward each year to ascending the hierarchy of roles. "I was looking forward to being one of the magi," one fourth-grader might say. Meanwhile there were more mundane reasons behind other people's complaints. The sets were already built for the old pageant and there were busy parents who were not interested in constructing new ones. What has happened here is that the pageant has taken on a life of its own. It is now part of the story of Advent in this particular congregation.

What does that imply for a pastor who has good reasons to change the script? It means that how the changes are introduced is as important as the changes themselves. For instance, there is a way to emphasize the continuity rather than the changes. Keeping the hierarchy of roles and maintaining the sets may be quite important. At the same time, changing the script itself may not be so controversial. In this way, the ritualized form of the pageant may well be more important to the congregation than are the actual words that the children speak. A significant part of a pastor's responsibility is to know the congregation well enough to understand

> How changes are introduced is as important as the changes themselves.

89

the symbolic meaning that people attach to regularized stories and ritualized activities.

Stories are so powerful that they can delude a congregation. My wife and I worshiped years ago in a congregation whose principal self-identity was as a "family congregation." But when we arrived the first time, we found almost no one in the sanctuary under retirement age. When the congregation's young pastor had a baby, the congregation decided to replace the furniture in the nursery because no one had used the furniture in so many years that it was no longer up to child safety codes. So how could a congregation almost devoid of families think of itself as a family congregation? It has to do with the story of the congregation's founding. It seems that in the 1940s or 1950s a woman named Alba Moore located the founding members of the congregation by walking the neighborhood looking for diapers hanging on backyard clotheslines. Wherever she found diapers, she knocked on the door and invited the family to the new church. Over the years, those families grew up. And, even if the kids have long-since moved away, some of those mothers still worship in the church. In fact, we discovered the power of the story one day when we sat in the pew belonging to the Smith family. Now, as far as I could tell, a geriatric woman named Mrs. Smith sat in that row each week all alone. And we thought we would be neighborly and sit next to her. We found out, however, that we had inadvertently invaded her space. You see, once or twice a year, her children and her grandchildren would come to visit and they would fill up the row. Just because those kids weren't coming this week or next did not give us the right to sit in their seats. That's the way most people in the congregation saw the world. In the minds of church folk, Mrs. Smith was simply a placeholder symbolizing the whole Smith family. In the end, the story became too powerful for the struggling congregation to overcome. When the pastor talked to the church board about making changes that would provide hospitality for young families that might visit, the board did not understand. "We are already a family church," they would reply, "so we really don't need to make any changes." The story of Alba Moore was so powerful that it defined them. Even when presented with data that showed that they were obviously no longer a church of families, they found ways to see what the story told them to see. They turned Mrs. Smith into the Smith family and they saw themselves as a church that welcomed young families because they themselves had been welcomed more than a generation ago. Their pastor was one of the most gifted preachers I have ever heard, but he could not get that congregation to hear anything that contradicted the story of Alba Moore.[50]

That is a negative example, showing how narratives can trap people. What about a positive example that shows the formative power of stories? The sociologist Robert Wuthnow investigated over the course of two books how people come to care for others. He looked, in *Acts of Compassion*, at adults engaged in volunteering[51] and asked, in *Learning to Care*, how children learn to be kind.[52] The common theme that he found in each of these studies was the importance of stories in cultivating kindness and inspiring volunteerism. *Acts of Compassion* focuses on how and why people perform selfless service while thriving in a society characterized by rugged individualism. He says that "having a language to describe our motives is one of the ways we make compassion possible in the individualistic society in which we live."[53] Yet when he examined this language of motivation, he did not find what we might expect. People did not talk about beliefs, values, or even purposes as resources for understanding their caring acts. "The accounts of our motives, when all is said, are basically stories," Wuthnow found "highly personalized stories, not assertions of high-flown values, but formulaic expressions of ourselves." We in the church often rely on theological beliefs or moral logics to muster people to action. He found instead that "It is not the language of religion or philosophy, or of psychology or economics, from which these accounts [of people's motivations] are constructed, but the language of personal experience." Wuthnow describes the paradigmatic account that a man named Jack Casey told of his motivation to serve. "Although he drew from various repertoires . . . he felt more comfortable telling a story. He had told it before. It brought together the deep anxieties of his inner being and the circumstances demanding a caring response in one dramatic episode."[54] Telling a story about one situation where he gave himself up for others was more compelling to him than mustering all the abstract beliefs, values, and purposes that surely fed into that decision to serve.

To solidify his point that "You cannot tell people what to do, you can only tell them parables,"[55] he examines the impact of one story of the American concept of compassion. He looks at how people understand Jesus' parable of the Good Samaritan.[56] He does a masterful job of showing how one story can mean many things to different people. When he asked people to retell the story in their own words, people recast the location so that it is the story of, say, a Communist on the Ho Chi Minh Trail or it is about a Mexican laborer. This change of context is important because it points to an important caveat in our discussion of why stories are so powerful. Wuthnow found that it was more important for a person to have seen the story lived out than it was for them to be able to tell the story. "Apparently the Good Samaritan parable is like other stories," Wuthnow found, "it cannot just be a part of historic lore to be relevant; it has to be revitalized, updated, put in your own context, for your actions to be influenced by it."[57] Stories thus need an interpreter, someone to update them with contemporary examples that bring the meaning of the story to life. That is why there is such a powerful tie between preaching and storytelling. They complement each other. And when a preacher helps people imagine themselves into a story, then they are motivated to live out that story in their daily lives. And that's how compassion becomes possible in an individualist society.

> Stories need an interpreter, someone to update them with contemporary examples that bring the meaning of the story to life.

But where did these adults learn to care? Wuthnow followed up his study by looking at how children and youth figure out how to put aside selfishness and pursue caring. The difficult transition for teens who are learning to express kindness in an impersonal society involves them moving from the "personalized caring they experience in their families" to the institutionalized care provided by churches and social service agencies. Once again, Wuthnow found that the power of stories was the key to this move toward compassionate action. Youth often feel trapped between two worlds—between selfishness and compassion, and between the personal world of family and the impersonal world of institutions. Thus teens do what all people do. When "we feel conflicted, we tell stories." These stories play out little dramas that allow us to experiment with new roles while maintaining our sense of personhood. Role models "enact our stories."[58] They "show us it is possible to perform well and still be human." Just as Jack Casey used stories to look backward and explain why he chose to serve others, teens use stories about role models to look into the future to imagine that they too could give of themselves. The stories then become an examination of the possible, a place to play with the future so that it no longer seems so daunting.[59]

Stories then become a wonderful resource for religious leaders who seek to lead by making meaning. There are a variety of ways to lead using stories. Let me give a couple of examples to illustrate them. First, stories allow leaders to instruct communities without being intrusive or singling people out for blame. I heard a wonderful example of this subtle leadership style while watching a baseball game on television a few years ago. Most of what I know about baseball, I learned from listening to Vin Scully narrate Dodger games. He wants his listeners not only to enjoy the game but also to come to appreciate the ways it was meant to be played. There are habits or actions that good players do as a matter of routine. And he wants people to understand and appreciate when players do things like "hit behind the runner" (i.e., when a batter sacrifices his own success so that a teammate can get to third base) or when a leadoff hitter "takes a strike" (the point is to give a breather to the pitcher who just batted so that the pitcher does not go to the mound winded).[60] Scully also would find ways to instruct listeners when a player was doing something foolish—that is, when a person violated the practices of good baseball. But it is the way that Scully taught about baseball that illustrates the power of meaning-making leadership. He told stories that created a context for interpreting the action. Many years ago, the Dodgers had a manager named Tommy Lasorda who seemed to enjoy drawing attention to himself, especially on national television. One night he trudged out to argue with an umpire when the call had obviously been correct. What was Scully to do? He did not want to embarrass the manager of his own team by saying that he was parading in front of the camera, but he also did not want to encourage the behavior that Lasorda was modeling. In this way, Scully faced a situation not unlike the one a pastor faces when a member of the staff or a prominent layperson makes a very public mistake. How do you correct the mistake without embarrassing the person who made it (especially if the person is not ready to acknowledge that it was a mistake)? Scully solved the problem by telling a story.

While the television showed Lasorda screaming at the umpire, Scully told a story. He talked about how he was just thinking of something that happened with Jackie Robinson, after he'd been in the league a few years. Jackie tried to steal second base and he was clearly out. But he leaped up and started arguing with the second base umpire. After a while, the manager came out to collect Jackie before the ump tossed him from the game. But that was not the end of it. Even in the locker room after the game Jackie complained to any reporter who would listen about how he was safe at second. Back in those days, he used to dress near an old Negro League player, one whose best years came long before they broke the color line. Eventually the old veteran had had enough. He turned Jackie's way and said in that gravelly voice of his, "Robinson, not only are you wrong, but you're loud wrong." Scully paused his story for a moment while Lasorda continued to shout. Then Scully simply repeated the phrase "loud wrong" and paused again while Lasorda's corpulent form filled the television screen. Just then the argument ended and up stepped the next Dodger hitter.[61] Without directly criticizing the Dodger manager, Scully had provided eloquent commentary on the event. His listeners were no doubt so entertained by the way that he told the story that most did not make a conscious connection to the events playing out on the screen in front of them. He couched it simply as a story about what happens when someone argues with an umpire. And the fact that he selected a story about the player who is easily the most revered Dodger in history cushioned whatever blow Lasorda might feel. After all, no one minds being put in the same story with Jackie Robinson. So there are lots of reasons why the story was gentle. But it nonetheless provided a context for interpreting the manager's behavior. He was "loud wrong" and that was embarrassing. The fact that as wonderful a role model as Jackie Robinson had once been loud wrong put him in good company. But the fact remains that there was a lesson to learn. No matter who you are, you can make a fool of yourself by arguing when the umpire is obviously correct. Scully gave a label to such bad baseball. And every time that I see someone foolishly arguing a call, I think that person is "loud wrong."

The usefulness of Scully's example does not, however, end there. Cultural resources often take on a life of their own. And, as often happens with a good story, it got repeated. I've told the story so many times that my wife knows it, even though she's not a baseball fan. More than once, she has asked me, after I complained about some situation or another, about whether or not I'm just being loud wrong. Once a phrase like that is established (i.e., legitimated) it can move throughout the lexicon of an organization—or a family.[62] Now, we use it to describe any moment when someone argues a point even though they are obviously wrong. Narratives have that kind of interpretative power.

And it is this interpretative power that is at the heart of meaning-making leadership. Let's return to the example we have been examining, wherein Charlotte Robinson writes a newsletter article in order to recruit teachers. She could indeed tell a poignant story that would motivate some congregants to volunteer. And she could expect to have some effect. But a more promising strategy would be to use a narrative form to intertwine a number of other cultural resources. She might say something like this, "The other morning I was eating a bagel at the counter in

> **Use a narrative form to intertwine a number of other cultural resources.**

Vargo's Diner when the woman on the next stool starting talking with me. On the television in the corner, a segment of *Good Morning America* came on about white supremacists from The Divine American Church of God. That's when she turned to me. 'Where did they learn such hatred?' she asked sadly, 'They weren't born that way.' I thought the question was rhetorical. So I just nodded in agreement. But that was not good enough for her. 'You're that new pastor in town, aren't you?' she said more strongly than I expected, 'Isn't the church teaching love anymore?' I tried to explain that not everyone who uses God's name is part of God's church. I was more defensive than I wanted to be. And I realized in the end that I was a bit embarrassed. We have a wonderful responsibility to bring up our congregation's children in the way of the Lord. But we have a problem—a pleasant problem, but a problem nonetheless. We now have too many children in Sunday school for our present structure to handle. So we are adding classes. And that means we need more teachers. Our congregation has always stepped up to fill the responsibilities entrusted to us. You did that long before I came as your pastor and you will continue to do it for years to come. That is part of what it means to be a member of this church. That's why this woman's questions are ringing in my ears, 'Where did they learn to hate?' and 'Where will they learn to love?' They can only learn if you are willing to teach them. Come and help our children learn the love of God."

Narratives are particularly powerful as cultural resources because they can weave all the other resources together into a coherent whole. The discourse around beliefs or values often has those resources standing alone. But narratives naturally pull in the other resources. Stories likewise can carry strong emotions, especially when the public narrative of a tradition (like Christianity) and the communal narrative of a people (like a congregation) come together to meet in an intensely personal story. The personal makes the public and communal narratives real. And the public and communal narratives validate the personal narratives. Narratives have such power because they operate simultaneously on so many levels. When these layers of meaning all cohere to speak the same message, narrative can be the most powerful cultural resource.

6. Practices as a cultural resource

The sixth cultural resource available to meaning-making leaders we will refer to as *practices*. These are the actions that define the very meaning of the church—the actions that the church and its members believe to express the heart of the faith. For example, many Christians believe that the most important thing a church does is worship. They are not referring to the Sunday morning worship service so much as the action that the service is supposed to enable—that is, paying homage to God. Worship, we Christians say, will outlast the earth. For, in the *eschaton*, the saints will spend eternity "casting down their golden crowns around the glassy sea."[63] The practice of worship has existed as long as there has been the church. It has changed its form as Christians the world over and through the centuries have found different ways to express devotion and respect to God. The practice, furthermore, is not a mere means to some larger end that would justify worship's existence. Worship is an end unto itself; it carries within itself the ultimate purpose for its own existence. Worship is thus a practice.

Let me give one more example before explaining the concept of practices in depth. Think of what happens when something terrible happens in a community. Say there is a tragic fire that swallows a family while they sleep. Or, to select a biblical example, say the Babylonian Empire is menacing the weakened nation-state of Judah, threatening to swallow it with its cruel implements of war. It is a moment that cries out for interpretation. We have talked about a lot of different resources on which a leader can draw as she makes sense of the situation. After the fire, for instance, the pastor can engage in a theological discussion of *theodicy* (explaining how such tragedy can happen under the watchful eye of a loving God), or she can refer to values or purposes as a way to mobilize the community to a caring response. We described in the last section how she could use stories to provide context or rituals to enable healing. But what is the very first thing that most pastors would say? Most pastors would not select any of these resources.

The first thing a pastor would do is to gather the community for prayer. Prayer communicates through a number of layers. It keeps us connected to God and expresses, primarily, our trust in God, even and especially in the face of tragedy. It allows us to place the lives of those who suffer in God's hands. And it enables the community to express its solidarity with those who grieve. But it also gives us a forum to go deeper. Prayer can be a place to challenge God. Rather than taking up detached theological arguments about theodicy, we can follow the biblical models that question God directly (I am thinking, for example, of the forthright psalms of lament or how the book of Habakkuk records Judah's frank indictment of God in the face of the Babylonian threat). And prayer allows us to take up these debates with God without abandoning the language of devoted trust. In other words, the practice of prayer contains within it the layers of meaning that a pastor would need to muster when she first encounters a tragedy.

Both worship and prayer are rather obvious examples. All Christians in all times and all places have participated in prayer and worship. Indeed, these practices characterize most religions in our world. So what is it about practices that are so special? And how are they different from other activities? For example, my congregation has a long-standing "practice" of shuttling elderly members to church in the church van. I would argue that such an activity is a wonderful thing to do. But it does not constitute a practice in the way that we will discuss it. We might say instead that it is part of the larger practice of hospitality. So far the distinction is nothing more than semantics. I call some things a practice and others don't qualify. Why go to the trouble of separating out some activities and calling them "practices"? And how does it change our understanding of leadership to look

> A practice can carry the multilayered weight of a community's competing commitments.

at practices? This section explains why and how a practice can carry the multilayered weight of a community's competing commitments—and why a meaning-making leader can and must build on Christian practices if she is to lead a Christian community.

This many-layered understanding of social practices draws on the writing of a philosopher named Alasdair MacIntyre, who laid out his ideas in a book called *After Virtue*.[64] There are four parts to his definition of practices that are particularly important if we are going to understand their depth. Understanding the ways that the parts of this definition reinforce each other is crucial to understanding how practices are different from other kinds of activities that a church might do. Practices (a) are communally defined, (b) are historically rooted within a tradition, (c) have what MacIntyre calls "internal goods" that embody the cardinal virtues of the tradition, and (d) have standards of excellence that separate formative engagement in a practice from destructive participation in the practice (with the key distinction being that formative engagement reinforces values and destructive participation erodes values). We will examine each of these parts in order.[65]

Practices are communally defined by and historically rooted within a tradition. An individual cannot, on her own, invent a practice. It does not become a practice until it becomes a regular part of the life of a community. This criterion separates MacIntyre's use of the term (and the usage we will adopt) from the common parlance on, for example, spiritual practices. As more individualistic concepts have erupted in American society, it has become fashionable in some religious environments to separate spirituality from religion—with the specific implication that spirituality does not depend on tradition in the ways that religion does.[66] Indeed, there are those who denigrate "religion" because they think it is tantamount to adhering to someone else's form of spirituality. I would argue, by contrast, that faith is a profoundly communal endeavor. When we pray or when we worship, we never stand alone. We are connected to the people of faith who have prayed to and worshiped God for thousands of years. And such connectedness is necessary to hold in check the human tendency for self-absorption. Attempts at practice that fail to include the community of faith have no checks and balances. And I believe that the human capacity for self-delusion is so profound that we need those restraints if we are going to do anything more than worship a projection of ourselves.[67] Practices must be communally defined and historically grounded.[68]

Practices also have internal goods. External goods are the collateral benefits that accrue from a practice. Mother Teresa gaining prestige in the world or a university making money are examples of external goods—because Mother Teresa did not help the poor in order to gain prestige and a university's reason for being is education not profit. Internal goods are those things that embody the cardinal virtues of a practice and achieve its ultimate ends. Every practice points to some virtue, some ultimate good that is so intertwined with the practice that excellent participation in the practice is tantamount to embodying the virtue. And each practice is a means to an end, but it is a means that is so closely tied to that end that the means cannot be separated from that end. The goal of the practice of discernment, for example, is to discover the will of God. When a person or community practices discernment well, then that person or community can proceed as if they have learned the will of God.[69]

Christian leaders bear a particular responsibility when it comes to the practices of the Christian faith. There is an always-present temptation toward entropy within a practice, where entropy is the tendency for a practice to become separated from the internal goods that are its beating heart. Take discernment, for example. When a leader initiates a discernment process, there is always a temptation to find the most expedient or the most advantageous outcome—rather than to seek the will of God. The mirrored temptation is to use the name discernment to refer to every decision-making process within the church. That is, to use the name discernment to baptize a congregation's every decision as the will of God. Entropy is so dangerous because it is self-deluding. It allows us to believe that we are embodying some ultimate good (such as finding the will of God) when in fact we have done nothing more than pursue what was right in our own eyes (to use the damning phrase from the book of Judges). That is why every practice has built into its historical development certain standards of excellence. Participation in a practice only embodies the internal goods of that practice when it adheres to the practice's standards of excellence.

The standards of excellence are the markers that separate productive participation from destructive participation in the practice. Destructive participation in the practice of discernment, for example, seeks to manipulate the outcome. It interferes with the practice and obscures the practice's ability to reveal God's will. In the same way, we can look at the earlier example of baseball, which many scholars use as a convenient way to talk about a nonreligious practice. When Vin Scully celebrates a player that "hits behind the runner" or breaks up a double play with a hard slide into second base, he is elevating the standards of excellence built into baseball. The phrase, "the way the game was meant to be played," is the shorthand that people use to describe these standards. The standards are often hidden from those who do not participate in the practice. So, for example, there are standards of excellence in baseball that are hidden from me, even though I am a fan. Sometimes I hear Joe Morgan (an announcer who was a Hall of Fame player) talk about the way that a hitter adjusted his shoulders as he swung in order to guide the ball into right field. But I just can't see it, even when Morgan explains it to me. I am not proficient enough in the practice of baseball to understand that standard of excellence.

This discussion comes back to Christian leadership because pastors often find themselves in exactly the role of the announcer. They are trying to explain a practice to the community of faith, but there will always be some people in the congregation who have not participated in the practice enough to understand what the preacher means. (And, the converse is also true; there will always be congregants who have a deeper

understanding of the practice than does the preacher who is trying to
explain it.) And that is where the analogy breaks down, because a pastor's
job is not just to explain a practice; it is also to inspire participation in
that practice. The preacher is to be both announcer and coach.

Take the practice of hospitality. God has exhorted God's people from
the earliest times to welcome the stranger, eventually adding the rationale ". . . for you were strangers in the land of Egypt" (Deut. 10:19b). The
practice of hospitality can take on many forms. We can see this in
Almond Springs. The congregation as a community welcomed Lazarus
and Dorcas Pha, Cambodian refugees with little more than the clothes on
their backs, into their midst in the 1970s. The community provided
material goods like food and clothing, they tutored the Pha children so
that they could catch up in school, and they included the family in every
congregational event. But one individual within the congregation took
that practice of hospitality a step deeper. Vic Vargo arranged for the couple to learn to be dry cleaners and then he opened a dry cleaning shop
specifically so that the Phas would have a livelihood. Vic confessed to his
pastor on his deathbed that he sometimes had to use profits from some of
his other businesses to prop up the dry cleaners. No one besides Vic's
daughter-in-law knew the extent to which he continued to provide for
the Phas decades after it seemed that he had exceeded the requirements
of hospitality. He understood at some deep level that the Phas would
always be strangers and would always need some kind of safety net. He
was looking out for their needs in ways that even they could not appreciate. And in so doing he was practicing hospitality.

As pastor of the Almond Springs
church, Charlotte Robinson was no
doubt aware of some of the ways that
this church practiced hospitality, but
unaware of others. Indeed, the congregation itself had likely forgotten
some of the ways that it had practiced
hospitality in the 1970s. This presents a problem and an opportunity for
a pastor like Charlotte. She has to
find a way to gather the stories about
the congregation's former practice

> The stories of past practice can become resources for enabling future practice.

and then create a means for communicating those stories back to the congregation. The stories of past practice can thus become resources for
enabling future practice.

These stories also become cautionary tales for discouraging destructive participation in the practice. For example, one of the members of the Almond Springs church, Margo Gold, does not trust her pastor, Charlotte Robinson. One of the reasons for this is that she sees Rev. Robinson as simply the next in a long line of pastors, none of whom could be trusted. Previous pastors usually made decisions without consulting the church board, but wrapped themselves in a blanket of faith by claiming that the decisions came from a process of "discernment." What is the pastor to do in such a situation, when someone has used a Christian practice destructively? One thing she can do is to create an objective standard that provides both a promise for new action and a guide for those who wish to evaluate it. That is where the practice of discernment could be a resource. One could imagine Charlotte teaching the church board about discernment, emphasizing the importance of listening to many voices. She could tell stories of how discernment only works when a person is willing to give up his initial assumptions and to be guided by the group. She could emphasize that the ultimate goal of discernment is not to get one's way but to seek out the will of God. And she could look to models from the history of the Christian faith to show how discernment has worked in the past. She could also tell specific stories of what she learned by listening to the church board.[70] By doing this, she can create a space where the board can together agree on a process for discerning what to do with the large bequest that has surprised the congregation. Understanding the four components of a practice (communally defined, historically rooted, aimed at internal goods, and following standards of excellence) allows a leader to use practices as a cultural resource.

Discernment is not the only practice that can be a resource for leading God's people.[71] Let me give two other examples of how practices enable meaning making. The first example focuses on a practice that is alive in practically every Christian church (baptism).[72] And the second shows the power of resurrecting a practice known throughout the church's history but not commonly seen in all churches today (anointing).

Many traditions do not think of baptism as a communal act, or if they do, they think of it as something that the individual does in the midst of the community of faith. But they tend not to think of the whole people of God as participating in the practice. I once heard a man explain why Presbyterians emphasize baptism's communal nature. He talked about the baptism of his daughter and how part of the service called for the congregation to make vows. The congregation promised to proclaim the faith to the children just as the parents promised to raise the child in the way of the Lord. The man went on to describe what happened many years later, after his child was grown. One night she called him from Denver, where she had gone to live. She told her father that she was in trouble. She had gotten into drugs and made a series of choices that she now regretted. She called asking him to help her turn her life around. But the man did not have a lot of options, a lot of resources. Circumstances were such that he could not move to Denver and she could not move back to his home. What was he to do? That night he called an old friend who now lived in Denver, a man who had been a part of the congregation that had promised at her baptism to proclaim the faith to her. He reminded his friend of that vow. And he asked his friend to honor that vow. He asked his friend to be the body of Christ for his daughter that night and in the months to come. His friend dropped what he was doing and attended to the girl and proclaimed the love of God to her when neither her father nor the institutional church could. When this man called on his friend he was drawing on the sacrament of baptism as a resource.

But the story does not end there. A few years ago I visited a friend who was a pastor in rural Virginia. She asked me to preach while I was in town. And it turned out that there was a baptism scheduled for that day. So I preached my standard baptism sermon—every minister probably has one. And in it I told the story of the daughter in Denver. I also talked about when my own daughter was baptized, just a few months before we moved across the country. I told them that the nature of the church is such that the congregation nurturing my daughter in California was now fulfilling the vows taken by the congregation that baptized her in Connecticut. After I preached this sermon, I discovered that the interpretation was far more meaningful for this Virginia congregation than I knew. The woman bringing the child for baptism was the child's grandmother and everyone knew that soon the child would be moving to a different part of the country. The congregation did not know quite what to make of such a nonstandard baptismal arrangement. What the sermon's stories said to that church was that they were taking a vow that another part of Christ's church would fulfill, just as they each day fulfill vows taken by other congregations. The magnificence of God's gift and magnitude of the church's vow left people in tears that day.

The very meaning of activities, such as Sunday school and youth work, changes when we see them in the context of the practices that they support and fulfill. If the pastor of that Virginia congregation had been in Charlotte's shoes and needed to recruit Sunday school teachers, she could have drawn on the vows that we take whenever a child is baptized. She could have described how those vows had been reinvigorated by the sacrament that the congregation enacted together. And that would have provided a basis for reinterpreting the very meaning of Sunday school teachers. Instead of volunteers who babysit kids while their parents worship (which was the dominant understanding in Almond Springs), she could say that Sunday school teachers are the people who fulfill each week the promise that we make every time a child is baptized.

That example illustrates how a very common practice can be a resource for the Christian leader. The next example shows how leaders can reinvigorate a practice and instill it with local meaning. The Bible is full of moments when people are anointed for new ministry. This happens with kings and with prophets. One pastor tells the story of how her church revived that practice while working with youth. Every year, before leaving on their annual mission trip, this pastor asked those who were participating in the trip to renew their baptism. They took their vows again and were then anointed with water from a bowl. This set them apart for the work of faith, and reminded them to embody the best of what those vows symbolize. Such a moment provides a tremendous opportunity to interpret the meaning of the mission trip for the youth (and for the congregation as a whole). It is tempting to see such a trip as just another youth activity, like a scavenger hunt or a trip to camp. And plenty of mission trips are indeed just that. But this anointing renewal of baptism might allow a leader to set the trip in a different framework. It sets the youth up as agents of reconciliation and ambassadors for Christ. And it recasts the church in the role of a sending church like the New Testament church at Antioch. A wealth of interpretative possibilities attend when we bring the practice of anointing to bear on youth who are leaving to minister in God's name.

Like the baptism story, however, there is more to the story, an incident that illustrates the tremendous meaning that comes from participating in Christian practices. The pastor who told this story talked about what happened some time after one of these mission trips. She and her husband had some kind of disagreement during dinner. Nothing serious, but everyone's mood was affected. Even her children were quiet. That evening, as she folded laundry in silence, her four-year-old son walked up to her with a bowl of water. "Mommy," he said, "I think you and Daddy need to renew your baptism." A four-year-old did that. That is the power of practices. Those who participate in them (and observe them) do not need to completely understand them.[73] But even a child can appropriate them. That boy tapped into a depth that he may have sensed but certainly did not understand. And in so doing he became a minister of reconciliation. In that moment, that young boy was a meaning-making leader.

A number of important themes come together in this example. In part 1, we talked about how action follows pre-legitimated paths and that people select from their repertoire of cultural tools when they construct meaning. This four-year-old did just that. He saw that the situation called for a renewal of something that had been lost. And he had seen that the practice of anointing had been used in another context to provide a forum for renewal and reconciliation. So he determined that the best path to renewal was through the practice. Of course, none of this calculus actually went through the boy's head as he decided what to do. It happened quite organically, almost instinctively. But that is the point. Observing and participating in the anointing services with the youth had worn a pathway in his experience. It said that if you want renewal, follow this path. So he did just that. He "transposed," to use Sewell's word,[74] the anointing ritual from an ecclesial context to one in his home. Or, to use the language we developed in part 1, once the practice was legitimated for him, he could use it for a purpose other than the one that originally legitimated it.

This example also illustrates the combined power of ritual and practice to reinforce each other's ability to make meaning. We have already discussed the way that ritual can encapsulate a story that can then be regularly enacted in the life of a community. Practices have a similar power. The practice of anointing—like most ritualized practices—has a narrative structure built into it. It is like a story in that it has a beginning, a middle, and an end. The beginning of the story is the prior action of the parties participating in the practice. In the case of anointing, it is the decision to present oneself for anointing (a decision, it should be noted, that neither the youth nor the parents of the four-year-old would have made apart from the prompting of a leader). The middle of the action is the ritual, which includes the actions that the participants take and the actions that God takes in that moment. And the end of the story is the future for which the ritualized practice prepares the participants. The narrative arc is like a pre-legitimated avenue for action in that the ritualized practice promises something in the future. In the case of anointing, the practice promises that the work done by the participant will have special significance because the person who serves has been set aside by God for the task. And the task, then, becomes more like a calling.[75] The practice of anointing illustrates the many layers of interpretation that even a child can tap into by using a practice to make meaning.

Practices are like narrative in that they incorporate the other cultural resources—and the other cultural resources are incorporated into the Christian practices. Practices can be seen in the "habits, virtues, knowledge, and other capacities of mind and spirit," in "biblical stories," and in "liturgical words and gestures," as well as the specific actions of the faith community.[76] This is the reason that practices can have so many layers of meaning.

One more thing needs to be said about practices as resources. A congregation needs to be engaged in faithful practice before a pastor can mobilize practices as a resource. If, to return to an earlier example, the only experience the Almond Springs congregation had of discernment involved manipulating a process to get one's way, then it would be unwise for a pastor to try to tap into discernment as a resource without rebuilding its meaning. Any practice can lose its integrity—that is, lose its tie to the values it is supposed to embody and the purposes it is to fulfill. If that happens, then the pastor has to work to restore the integrity of the practice before it can be used in a meaningful way. Charlotte Robinson faces just that dilemma in Almond Springs. Before she arrived as pastor, the congregation had not emphasized any practices. They did things that pointed to practices, but they did not maintain the integrity of the practice. For example, the congregation practiced hospitality in the way that it welcomed visitors. But there was a limit to its practice. The congregation did not do a good job welcoming people who were ethnically different. In the 1970s, they may have welcomed a Cambodian refugee family. But Charlotte knows that in present times they would not extend the same courtesy to a family of migrant farm workers. Indeed, Chris Argyris's language might again be helpful here. You will recall that he distinguished between "espoused theory" and "theory in use." In this case, the Almond Springs congregation had an espoused practice of hospitality but they could not always put it to use. Charlotte Robinson found that the same was true of most of the practices when she arrived in Almond Springs.

Throughout this discussion of cultural resources, we have repeatedly returned to the example of how Charlotte Robinson could mobilize

> A congregation needs to be engaged in faithful practice before a pastor can mobilize practices as a resource.

cultural resources in order to recruit Sunday school teachers. Each of the illustrations has shown how one particular resource (such as, say, values) could be used to reframe how congregants see the possibility of teaching. It seems appropriate now to culminate the example by showing how the pastor might write a letter that weaves together each of the cultural resources into a coherent interpretive whole. This will be a particularly interesting exercise because Rev. Robinson faces a common dilemma in that her congregation has a limited understanding of many of the practices that characterize Christian faith. So part of her task might be to begin a process of pouring new meaning into a practice, namely the practice of teaching. With that said, she might write something like this.

"There is no greater privilege for a church than to pass the Christian faith on to the next generation. And there is no greater responsibility. When a child internalizes the faith, she begins to see the world through Christian eyes. Ask the schoolteachers in our midst—people like Ansel Richards or Laura Webber—about the selfish temptations that inundate our kids. And then ask them where those kids find the inspiration to resist those temptations. I am not just talking about drugs and sex. I have in mind something more insidious. How do kids learn, for example, not to be selfish? Where do they get the inspiration? One way they learn is by following the example of their parents. And another way they learn is by coming to church. We all believe that attending church is good for a child's soul. But how exactly does the church help children become better human beings? One way is by teaching those children. We teach them that God loves them, that Jesus sacrificed himself for them, and that God's Holy Spirit lives within them. We teach them about kindness and gentleness. And we help them see, through projects like One Great Hour of Sharing, that they can make a difference in the world. How do we do that? Well, we spend most of our time telling stories to the children. They learn, for example, about the Good Samaritan. And that's where they learn to care for others, even those who are not like themselves. And that's how our kids become the kind of adults who will make a difference in the world. Come help us shape a child's world so that they see it through Christian eyes."

We have discussed many different cultural resources. Belonging allows people to separate insiders from outsiders and to say, "We are the kind of people who . . . " Theology shapes people by changing the ideas that they use to construct their actions. Values give people a set of behaviors to which they can aspire. Goals carve paths for people by giving them something to accomplish in the world. Stories provide a framework for putting events into a coherent structure that ties together the past, the present, and the future. And practices allow people to take actions that encapsulate the ends to which they aspire. By putting all these together, a pastor can change the way that her congregation sees the world. And by changing the ways that a congregant sees the world, the pastor can change the very world in which that person lives.

Notes

1. It should be noted that the sermon is not the focal point of worship services in every Christian tradition. Liturgical traditions especially deemphasize the sermon. But that does not limit the pastor's power. A ten-minute homily can have the same long-term effect as a twenty-minute sermon. Likewise, the more conservative Protestant traditions that ask the pastor to preach for forty-five minutes or more only increase the pastor's authority by a marginal amount.

2. I should also note that cultural resources could be of tremendous advantage to leaders who do not preach. I emphasize the sermon, however, because it is such an obvious example. The model that we will use throughout part 2—a leader's article in the organizational newsletter—would be available to a range of leaders.

3. For a particularly wise example of how the calling of a minister is inextricably linked to his interpretative responsibilities, see any of Eugene H. Peterson's reflective books, especially, *Working the Angles: The Shape of Pastoral Integrity* (Grand Rapids, Mich.: Eerdmans, 1987), *Under the Unpredictable Plant: An Exploration in Vocational Holiness* (Grand Rapids, Mich.: Eerdmans, 1992); and Peterson and Marva Dawn, *The Unnecessary Pastor: Rediscovering the Call* (Grand Rapids, Mich.: Eerdmans, 2000).

4. My thoughts on the amount of time it takes for ideas to grow are strongly influenced by Heifetz's understanding of "pacing." See Ronald Heifetz, *Leadership Without Easy Answers*, esp. chapter 4.

5. For an insightful discussion of the momentum that change creates as it builds upon itself, see Jim Collins, *Good to Great* (New York: HarperBusiness, 2001), esp. chapter 8.

6. Rhys Williams argues that "rhetoric and ideology can be thought of as 'cultural resources' and analyzed in many of the same ways as are the more conventional 'structural' resources of money, members, and organizations." Williams, "Constructing the Public Good: Social Movements and Cultural Resources," *Social Problems* 42, no. 1 (February 1995): 125.

7. The most interesting recent article-length discussion of social structure is William Sewell, "A Theory of Structure: Duality, Agency, and Transformation," *American Journal of Sociology* 98 (1992): 1–29.

8. On the "cultural power" that derives from cultural resources, see Rhys Williams and N. J. Demerath, "Cultural Power: How Underdog Religious and Nonreligious Movements Triumph Against Structural Odds," in *Sacred Companies*, eds. Demerath et al. (New York: Oxford University Press, 1998), 364–78.

9. The distinction between this paragraph and the previous one turns on the difference between power and authority. A simple way to explain the distinction is that power is the ability to impose one's will, while authority is the prerogative to determine an outcome. In theory, power's ability is tightly bound to authority's prerogative. But we all know that is not always the case. In the Almond Springs case, Charlotte (the pastor) is the supervisor of Mavis (the secretary). She has that authority. And that means she has the prerogative to tell Mavis not to discuss church business with other people. But she does not have the power to make Mavis keep quiet. The pastor can fire the secretary, but short of that she has little recourse. This distinction is important because religious leaders often confuse power and authority. They sometimes think that being assigned the authority will give them the power, which is not always the case. And they sometimes think that they lack power because they do not have authority. Having authority does not ensure power; just as lacking authority does preclude power.

10. John Kotter of the Harvard Business School draws a distinction between management and leadership on just this point. He concludes that, "good management controls complexity [while] effective leadership produces useful change." His work is one of many recent examples where management scholars are arguing that the controlling model that has dominated business education must give way to a model of interpretation and inspiration. No less an authority than Peter Drucker proclaims that the new model for leadership can be found in the churches, where "mission" is more important than "expediency" and "accountability" more prevalent than "control." Kotter, "What Leaders Really Do," *Harvard Business Review* (May-June 1990): 3–11. Drucker, "What Business Can Learn from Nonprofits," *Harvard Business Review* (July-August 1989): 88–93.

11. This control model may be losing its efficacy even in the business world. For example, Peter Drucker has observed that the "post-capitalist executive" will have to learn to lead without relying on the trappings of hierarchical power. "You have to learn to manage in situations where you don't have command authority, where you are neither controlled or controlling. That is the fundamental change." Drucker, "The Post-Capitalist Executive: An Interview with Peter Drucker," *Harvard Business Review* (May-June 1993): 115, quoted in Jay A. Conger, *Winning 'Em Over: A New Model for Managing in the Age of Persuasion* (New York: Simon & Schuster, 1998), 180; cf. Conger, "The Necessary Art of Persuasion," *Harvard Business Review* (May-June 1998): 84–95.

12. The sociological distinction between culture and structure is an important part of this analysis. Structure describes categories and characteristics that are formal and often unchanging. Authority assigned by law (e.g., the authority of a police officer) and demographic characteristics such as gender and age are structural categories. They are open to very little interpretation (granting the degree to which some might want to reinterpret gender as a category). Cultural characteristics, by contrast, rely almost solely on interpretation for their meaning. Authority may be assigned, for example, but it does not always translate to power (as any pastor will tell you). On the distinctions between structure and culture specifically as they apply to religion's power and authority, see N. J. Demerath and Rhys Williams, *A Bridging of Faiths: Religion and Politics in a New England City* (Princeton, N.J.: Princeton University Press, 1992), esp. 170–72, 284–86.

13. This section draws heavily on ideas that I have detailed in my dissertation, which asked how voluntary associations (secular and religious) created solidarity and built commitment in turn-of-the-century urban America. I found that voluntary associations structured their members' lives around ethnic loyalty, brotherhood, sisterhood, and class-consciousness in just the same way that churches organized their members' lives around faith. My use of the term "cultural resources" derives from Rhys Williams's work on the means by which social movements propagated. I have expanded his original discussion of ideology as a cultural resource, and made ideology one among many cultural resources that I found at work among voluntary associations a century ago. See especially Williams, "Social Movement Theory and the Sociology of Religion: 'Cultural Resources' in Strategy and Organization" PONPO Working Paper #180, Program on Non-Profit Organizations, (Yale University, 1993); Scott Cormode, "Faith & Affiliation: An Urban Religious History of Churches and Secular Voluntarism in Chicago's West Town, 1871–1914," unpublished dissertation (Yale University, 1996); Rhys Williams, "Constructing the Public Good: Social Movements and Cultural Resources," *Social Problems* 42, no. 1 (February 1995): 124–44.

14. James Hopewell, *Congregation: Stories and Structure* (Philadelphia: Fortress Press, 1987), 4, 5, and 7.

15. My thinking on this point draws on work from social movement theory and neo-institutionalist organization theory combined with the widely used but under-theorized notion that culture works like a tool kit. With the neoinstitutionalists, I emphasize the idea of legitimation (what DiMaggio calls "cultural entrepreneurship") as the means by which new cultural resources are made available for public use. From Swidler, I take the idea that once cultural symbols are legitimated they can be wielded like tools—that is, separated from or "loosely coupled" with the logics that originally legitimated them. And, from the social movement theorists, I learned that these pre-legitimated symbols and systems of thought could become "resources" that may be used to mobilize a group or justify an action. On culture as tool kit, see Ann Swidler, "Culture in Action: Symbols and Strategies," *American Sociological Review* 51 (1986): 273–86; On neoinstitutionalism, see Paul DiMaggio, "Cultural Entrepreneurship in Nineteenth-Century Boston," *Media, Culture and Society*, 33–50; Paul DiMaggio and Walter Powell, "The Iron Cage Revisited: Institutional Isomorphism and Collective Rationality," *The New Institutionalism in Organizational Analysis*, 63–82 (see part 1, n. 44); on "logics," see Roger Friedland and Robert R. Alford, "Bringing Society Back In: Symbols, Practices, and Institutional Contradictions," in Powell and DiMaggio, 232–63, and Harry Stout and Scott Cormode, "Institutions and the Story of American Religion: A Sketch of a Synthesis" in Demerath et al., *Sacred Companies*; and on "social movement ideology as a set of 'cultural resources,'" see Rhys Williams, "Rhetoric, Strategy, and Institutionalization: Social Movements and Cultural Resources," paper presented to the annual meeting of the Society for the Scientific Study of Religion, Washington, D.C., October 1992.

16. For further discussion of the concept of cultural resources and a discussion of how cultural resources relate to nineteenth century religious and secular voluntary associations, see Scott Cormode, "Faith & Affiliation: An Urban Religious History of Churches and Secular Voluntarism in Chicago's West Town, 1871–1914."

17. An earlier description of the implications of cultural resources for leadership appears in Scott Cormode, "Leading with Cultural Resources: Management Lessons from

Voluntary Associations," unpublished paper presented to the Research Colloquium, Peter F. Drucker Graduate Management Center (April 1997).

18. Robert Wuthnow has shown that the salience of denominational loyalty has eroded significantly in the last half-century. It was once true that other cultural resources (esp. beliefs and values) were closely tied to denominational identity. So if you told me that you were a Methodist, I would know a lot about what you believed and what values you hoped to embody. That is no longer the case. If you were to sit down in a random United Methodist church today, the denominational identity of the congregation would do little to help you predict the beliefs of the people sitting next to you in the pew. Wuthnow, *Restructuring of American Religion* (Princeton, N.J.: Princeton University Press, 1988); to compare Wuthnow's study to studies that show that in the nineteenth century there was a strong connection among denominational identity, class location, ethnic identity, beliefs, values, and practices, see for example, Donald Harrison Doyle, *The Social Order of a Frontier Community: Jacksonville, Illinois, 1825–1870* (Urbana, Ill.: University of Illinois Press, 1978).

19. Ammerman, *Congregation & Community*, pp. 34ff (see part 1, n. 56).

20. See, for example, the descriptions of the so-called "emergent church movement." These churches are particularly effective at providing hospitality to people who are uncomfortable in the traditional church. For example, they have very different norms that govern their liturgical and sacramental practices. The practice of communion, for example, in such congregations is quite different from the way it is practiced in denominationally traditional congregations. That is part of the draw of such congregations. By the same token, folk who are at home in the traditional church might feel unwelcome in one of these emergent congregations. The very attitudes and practices that welcome one segment of the population would offend another group.

21. Ammerman discussed this when commenting on the research behind her *Congregation & Community* book. She said that one of the measures of healthy congregations was the extent to which a church provided a means for outsiders to understand the congregation as an insider would—i.e., provided a mechanism to transform outsiders into insiders. Ammerman, "Skills and Competencies for Managing Internal and External Environments," unpublished paper presented to Yale University's National Seminar on Religious Leadership (January 22, 1999).

22. The idea here is to make insiders by pretending that your group is composed of outsiders struggling against a dominant majority. This counterintuitive idea turns out to be quite common in the history of American faith. The historian R. Laurence Moore has shown that many faith traditions followed this path, including the Mormons, the Jews, the Catholics, the Evangelicals, and even the established Protestant Mainline. Each one rallied its people by showing how it was a group of outsiders. See *Religious Outsiders and the Making of Americans* (New York: Oxford University Press, 1986).

23. Note that for the purposes of explanation, this section purposely draws the distinctions between Evangelicals and Mainline Protestants in broad strokes. Any one person from either of these perspectives will likely be more nuanced in their perspective.

24. Part of the reason for delineating the differences between Evangelicals and Mainline Protestants is that Wuthnow has shown that denominational loyalty has been replaced by two cultural poles, one conservative and the other liberal. We said earlier that denominational identity did not predict much about a person's belief. On the other hand, knowing whether a person identified with one or the other of the poles would allow one

to predict quite a bit about the person's beliefs, values, and practices. Wuthnow, *Restructuring of American Religion*.

25. Brief Statement of Reformed Faith, Presbyterian Church (USA), line 37.

26. NB: Rev. Robinson's comment also reinforces the notion that Almond Springs Presbyterian Church thinks of itself as a parish congregation. The church feels a responsibility to the town itself.

27. I include the term *ideology* because this cultural resource is important even to secular leaders. For example, Peter Drucker writes that each business leader should understand the "theory of the business." See Drucker, "Theory of the Business," *Harvard Business Review* (September-October 1994): 95–104.

28. Williams and Demerath, "Cultural Power (see n. 8)."

29. On the teaching office itself, see Richard Osmer, *A Teachable Spirit: Recovering the Teaching Office in the Church* (Westminster/John Knox Press, 1990).

30. All of this is particularly ironic, of course, because the politics that characterize these groups tend to go in the opposite directions—as we will see when discussing the fourth cultural resource. Religious conservatives tend to be political conservatives. And political conservatives argue for less government intervention and more in the way of personal freedom (except on issues of morality). Likewise, religious liberals tend to be political liberals. And political liberals argue for a greater role for government to protect rights and to ensure tolerance. The most notable exception to these sweeping generalizations is, of course, the liberal evangelical movement that is both theologically conservative and socially liberal. This group argues for an agenda that one of its spokespersons calls "completely pro-life." They oppose both war and abortion. They favor multiculturalism and cross-cultural evangelism. The views of this group can be seen in authors such as Ronald Sider and Tony Campolo.

31. There are, of course, congregations that take the opposite approach. Some congregations quote Martin Luther, who famously called the book of James an "epistle of straw" specifically because it seemed to elevate actions to be on the same level with faith (James 2:14-19).

32. There are some who chafe at the idea that worship is directed internally. They argue that true worship focuses on God and not on the self. As such, any worship that is internally directed is not really worship. I grant the point. But I don't mean *internally directed* to mean "focused on self." What I mean is that true discipleship must take the Christian beyond the walls of the sanctuary and into a world that needs to hear God's message of hope. So feel free to translate my use of the phrase *internally directed* so that it means "action that takes place cloistered from the secular world." You can likewise take *externally directed* to mean "action for the sake of and in the midst of the secular world." Examples of internally-directed activities are worship, teaching, administration, and fellowship. Examples of externally-directed activities are evangelism, peacemaking, visiting the sick, prison ministries, and feeding the poor.

33. Comparing the formative power of ideas to that of narratives, Robert Wuthnow has said, "How we think about ethical questions is of enormous importance, but our thinking is less likely to be shaped by the abstract claims of the philosopher than by the concrete tutelage of the storyteller." Wuthnow, "Stories to Live By," *Theology Today* 49, no. 3 (October 1993): 297.

34. On the importance of a "constitutive narrative," see the discussion of "communities of memory" in Bellah, et al., *Habits of the Heart*, (N.Y.: Harper & Row, 1985), 125ff.

35. Jerome Bruner, "Life as Narrative," *Social Research* 54 (1987): 31, quoted in Robert Wuthnow, "Stories to Live By," 307.

36. Nancy T. Ammerman, "Religious Identities and Religious Institutions" in *Handbook of the Sociology of Religion*, ed. Michele Dillon (New York: Cambridge University Press, 2003), 207-24.

37. Margaret Somers identifies four kinds of narrative. Somers, "The Narrative Construction of Identity: A Relational and Network Approach," *Theory and Society* 23 (1994): 605-49, quoted in Ammerman, "Religious Identities."

38. James Hopewell describes how churches access these public narratives: "A congregation, undeniably Christian, nevertheless uses forms and stories common to a larger world treasury to create its own local religion of outlooks, action patterns, and values." Hopewell, *Congregation: Stories and Structure*, 3.

39. The story eventually took on a mythic quality for me as well. One of my most vivid memories of the experience involves lying on the examination table in my pediatrician's office while the intern examined my head. I recall seeing her spray orange drops of Betadine onto the wall as she prepared the wound for stitching. And every time I returned to that pediatrician's office throughout my youth, I looked on the wall for the stains those drops made. I remember telling people that I saw them. With the clarity of an adult, I realize that I probably did not see exactly the stains made from my visit. I am sure that the wallpaper in those exam rooms experienced many such stains. As a child, however, the sight of something tangible like the stains on the wall reinforced my faith by calling to mind this formative religious experience. Indeed, there is research that suggests that having something material reinforces the memory of an experience. This is the reason, for example, that teens buy concert T-shirts. And this is why rituals support religious memory. On the connection between tangible mementos and experiences, see Joseph Pine and James Gilmore, *The Experience Economy* (Cambridge, Mass.: Harvard Business School Press, 1999); on the connection between ritual, narrative, and memory, see Herbert Anderson and Edward Foley, *Mighty Stories, Dangerous Rituals* (San Francisco: Jossey-Bass, 1998).

40. Anderson and Foley argue that narratives create a "transformative encounter" between the human and divine. "We are transformed in part because we begin to understand our particular story as part of a larger, transcendent story" (p. 37). This is why they can conclude that, "we create stories and live according to their narrative assumptions" (p. 6). Anderson and Foley, *Mighty Stories*.

41. Similar narrative structures exist for Mainline Protestants. When I taught at a Methodist seminary, most of the students talked about their "journey of faith." This image of journey gives them a plot line to describe their ongoing process of discovery. It says to them that every point on the journey is as important as every other. And it presumes that there is not a particular destination toward which the journey moves. The image gives them a way to tell their own story without making judgments about the validity of other people's journeys or about the necessity for coherence between their present understanding of God and any constructions that they subscribed to in the past.

42. I now prefer to draw on language of "belonging to God" that is similar to the first question/answer to the Heidelberg Catechism, which says, "Q1: What is your only comfort in life and in death? A1: That I belong—body and soul, in life and in death—not to myself, but to my faithful savior, Jesus Christ."

43. Discounting this flexibility has endangered the church before. The historian James Turner has shown, for example, that unbelief (i.e., the idea that there is no God) became

accepted in American culture because nineteenth-century Protestants proclaimed a God that looked like a respectable Victorian gentleman. And when Victorian gentlemen passed from vogue at the turn of the century, they took God's credibility with them. Turner, *Without God, Without Creed* (Baltimore: Johns Hopkins Press, 1985).

44. Wuthnow, "Church Realities and Christian Identity in the 21st Century," *Christian Century* (May 12, 1993): 520–23.

45. The best summary of how religious identity takes a necessarily narrative form is Ammerman, "Religious Identities and Religious Institutions," *Handbook of the Sociology of Religion*, ed. Michelle Dillon (Cambridge: Cambridge University Press).

46. Anderson and Foley, *Mighty Stories*, 11.

47. Anderson and Foley, *Mighty Stories*, 27, 25.

48. The converse applies as well. They use arguments that social liberals usually muster to oppose capital punishment in order to oppose abortion as well. Ronald Sider, *Completely Pro-Life: Building a Consistent Stance* (Downers Grove, Ill.: Inter-Varsity Press, 1987).

49. Any given ritual or narrative can make a range of different meanings. "The expressive character of ritual permits or groups with different claims on the larger collective order to articulate their own position in relation to the moral order...Narrative also permits multiple layers of meaning to be communicated to the same person or group, thereby enriching the significance of the ritual itself and ensuring a more dramatic and sustained impact on its participants." Wuthnow, *Meaning and Moral Order: Explorations in Cultural Analysis* (Berkeley: University of California Press, 1987), 136.

50. Pastoral care professionals often talk about how people can get trapped within a story that they allow to define them. On ways to escape such as situation, see Anderson and Foley, *Mighty Stories*, chapter 7, "New Rituals."

51. Wuthnow, *Acts of Compassion: Caring for Others and Helping Ourselves* (Princeton, N.J.: Princeton University Press, 1991).

52. Wuthnow, *Learning to Care: Elementary Kindness in an Age of Indifference* (New York: Oxford University Press, 1995).

53. Wuthnow, *Acts of Compassion*, 49, 50.

54. Wuthnow, *Acts of Compassion*, 84, 85.

55. Wuthnow is quoting the poet and essayist W. H. Auden, "Art and Psychology," in *The Arts Today*, ed. Geoffrey Grigson (London: John Lane, 1935): 18, quoted in Wuthnow, *Acts of Compassion*, 179.

56. Wuthnow, *Acts of Compassion*, chapter 6: "Along the Road," 157–87.

57. Wuthnow, *Acts of Compassion*, 162. (Note: Wuthnow adds, "Fortunately, most people—85 percent—who can tell the story have also experienced an example of it in their lives.")

58. Wuthnow, *Learning to Care*, 132–34.

59. Wuthnow actually lists quite a few ways that storytelling motivates young people to selfless service. For example, in *Learning to Care*, he says that storytelling "brings something abstract down to earth so that it can be understood at several levels, viscerally as well as intellectually" (p. 137). It makes "events more relevant to the context in which people live" (p. 137). Stories "show that caring need not involve great sacrifice or heroism but can be demonstrated in small acts of kindness" (p. 138). Indeed, he found that stories of great heroes like Mother Teresa "were too distant from [teen's] own experience to be meaningful" and it is "mundane stories [that] make caring possible" (p. 139). Stories

also "encapsulate a sense of belonging" that demonstrate how caring institutions like a church can provide "a halfway house, a home away from home, where bonds can develop similar to those of one's family" (p. 140). "Storytelling also resolves the contradictions we experience as we move into institutional roles, by convincing us that we are still whole persons rather than becoming nothing more than the roles we play" (p. 141).

60. These are exactly the behaviors that, in the next section, we will call "goods internal to the practice" of baseball. For an insightful explanation of practices using baseball as an example, see Jeffrey Stout, *Ethics After Babel: The Languages of Morals and Their Discontents* (Boston: Beacon Press, 1988), 276ff.

61. This is my memory of the story as I heard it. I want to thank the publicity staff of the Los Angeles Dodgers for confirming the story with Mr. Scully.

62. This is what Sewell, following Bourdieu, means by transposability. Cultural resources can be transferred or transposed into contexts beyond the ones that originally defined them. For an example of how transposability affects the relationship between religion and race, see Michael Emerson and Christian Smith, *Divided By Faith: Evangelical Religion and the Problem of Race in America* (New York: Oxford University Press, 2000), esp.75ff. They note that "people not only employ their cultural tools in the context in which they were first learned, but transpose or extend them to new and diverse situations. Thus, evangelicals, like others, use their religio-cultural tools not only in directly religious contexts, but in helping them make sense of issues like race relations" (p. 76). Sewell, "Theory of Structure," 17 (see n. 7), referencing Pierre Bourdieu, *Outline of a Theory of Practice* (Cambridge, Mass.: Cambridge University Press, 1977), 83.

63. "Holy, Holy, Holy! Lord God Almighty," words by Reginald Heber, 1826.

64. MacIntyre's writing is itself rather opaque. So much of the material that I will quote to explain his ideas will come from his students and others who have used his work to good effect. You will understand why it is necessary to rely so heavily on his interpreters when I give you his definition of a practice. A social practice is "any coherent and complex form of socially established cooperative human activity through which good internal to that form of activity are realized in the course of trying to achieve those standards of excellence which are appropriate to, and partially definitive of, that form of activity, with the result that human powers to achieve excellence, and human conceptions of the ends and goods involved, are systematically extended." Alasdair MacIntyre, *After Virtue* (Notre Dame, Ind: University of Notre Dame Press, 1984 [1981]), 187.

65. The concept of practice has slightly different meanings in the various scholarly traditions. Religious educators, for instance, distinguish between theory and practice, especially emphasizing the fallacy of assuming that theory always precedes practice. Sociologists also have a different take on the word *practice*. They see "'practice' as [any] unconscious, embodied, or habitual action, contrasted with articulated, conscious ideas." The quote is from Swidler, *Talk of Love*, 191, but she references Stephen Turner and others as well. Other important sociological discussions of practice come from Michel Foucault—who emphasizes the ways that practices replicate and reinforce power structures—and Pierre Bourdieu, who insists that "practice has a logic which is not that of the logician." On Foucault, see for example, *The History of Sexuality* (New York: Pantheon, 1978); Pierre Bourdieu, *The Logic of Practice* (Stanford: Stanford University Press, 1990), quoted in Swidler, 192; cf. Wuthnow et al., *Cultural Analysis: The Work of Peter L. Berger, Mary Douglas, Michel Foucault, and Jurgen Habermas* (London: Routledge and Kegan Paul, 1984); and Stephen Turner, *The Social Theory of Practices: Tradition, Tacit Knowledge, and*

Presuppositions (Chicago: University of Chicago Press, 1994); cf., on "logics," Roger Friedland and Robert Alford, "Bringing Society Back In: Symbols, Practices, and Institutional Centralizations," in Powell and DiMaggio, *The New Institutionalism*, 223–62; on an application of Friedland and Alford's notion of "institutional logics" to the world of faith, see Harry S. Stout and Scott Cormode, "Institutions and the Story of American History: A Sketch of a Synthesis," in Demerath et al., *Sacred Companies*, 62–78.

66. The most famous form of this radically individualized spirituality has come to be called "Sheilaism." It is so named because Robert Bellah and his coauthors write about a woman who describes her faith by referring to herself. "My faith has carried me along," she said, "It's Sheilaism. Just my own little voice." Then, when asked to define this faith, she said, "It's just try to love yourself and be gentle with yourself. You know, I guess, take care of each other." Bellah et al., *Habits of the Heart*, 221 (see n. 34); see also Wade Clark Roof, *A Generation of Seekers: The Spiritual Journeys of the Baby Boom Generation* (New York: HarperSanFrancisco, 1993), which emphasizes the contemporary tendency for some to say that they are "spiritual but not religious."

67. It is important, of course, to recognize that practices can become trapped by tradition. The community of faith must reinvent and reinvigorate a practice with each new generation. This debate mirrors the biblical balance that avoids the poles of legalism and antinomianism. John Calvin, according to the historian William Bouwsma, described this as walking between the labyrinth and the abyss. The labyrinth represented the over-dependence on rules, law, and tradition. He does not use the term the way that some contemporary Christians talk of "walking the labyrinth." Instead, he referred to a place where the walls close in and the way out is hidden behind layers of confusing passages. The abyss, on the other hand, represents the lack of boundaries and guidance. It refers to the feeling of never-ending free-fall that comes when one cannot get oriented and is left to conjure one's own construction of God and the world. I would argue that people who participate in Christian practices are constantly walking between the labyrinth of stale traditionalism and the abyss of traditionlessness. William Bouwsma, *John Calvin: A Sixteenth Century Portrait* (New York: Oxford University Press, 1988), 45.

68. Robert Wuthnow has proposed a framework for spirituality based on practices. He observes that "a traditional spirituality of inhabiting sacred places has given way to a new spirituality of seeking—that people have been losing faith in a metaphysic that can make them feel at home in the universe and that they increasingly negotiate among competing glimpses of the sacred, seeking partial knowledge and practical wisdom" (p. 3). To this group, he proposes a "the idea of a practice-oriented spirituality" (p. 168). Wuthnow, *After Heaven: Spirituality in America since the 1950s* (Berkeley: University of California Press, 1998).

69. One caveat on discernment is that practicing it well means that we are never so confident in our succss that we stop listening for future direction from God.

70. The pastor in such a situation should not, however, expect people to change quickly. Only when they have seen the pastor practice discernment correctly will they begin to adopt the meaning that the pastor has tried to create with her teaching. On this point, see Karl Weick, "Small Wins: Redefining the Scale of Social Problems," *American Psychologist*, 39, no. 1 (1984): 40–49.

71. There is, of course, no definitive list of Christian practices. But there some helpful lists that can serve as the starting point for reflection. Craig Dykstra lists fourteen "practices that appear consistently throughout the tradition and that are particularly significant

for Christians today." These include: worship, reading Scripture, interpreting Scripture, praying, confession, encouragement and exhortation, service, giving, suffering, hospitality, listening, learning "about the context in which we live," resisting [evil], building life-sustaining structures and institutions. Note that for the sake of brevity that I have not used Dykstra's exact formation in listing these. The most important thing that my abbreviation leaves out is the helpful way that he emphasizes the communal nature of practices by incorporating the word together into almost all the descriptive formulations. Dykstra, *Growing in the Life of Faith* (Louisville, Ky.: Geneva Press, 1999), 42, 43; other lists exist in Kenda Creasy Dean, *Practicing Passion: Youth and the Quest for a Passionate Church* (Grand Rapids, Mich.: Eerdmans, 2004), 154, 155; at least a portion of Dean's analysis is dependent on Dykstra.

72. There are those who would distinguish a practice from a sacrament like baptism.` That is helpful to the extent that it reminds us that God's action stands at the core of a sacrament. But, for the purposes of this section, a sacrament can be a resource for the meaning-making leader in exactly the same way that a practice can. So I have chosen not to emphasize the distinction here.

73. Indeed, none of us ever will completely understand the depths of the practices.

74. Sewell, "Theory of Structure," 17.

75. One of the things that particularly appeals to me about the story of anointing the youth is that they get a foretaste of vocation. It is often hard to help young people understand the difference between a calling and any other act of service. If used properly and not arbitrarily, the practice of anointing can enable youth to see that one is chosen for a calling (sometimes even drafted), that a calling requires preparation, that a calling transforms the nature of one's labors, and that a calling involves divine action mediated through human sources.

76. Craig Dykstra and Dorothy C. Bass, "A Theological Understanding of Christian Practices," in *Practicing Theology: Beliefs and Practices in Christian Life*, ed. Miroslav Volf and Dorothy C. Bass (Grand Rapids, Mich.: Eerdmans Publishing Company, 2002), 19.

CHRISTIANITY AND MONEY

The purpose of this conclusion is to show in detail how the ideas and principles developed in this book apply to a particularly difficult problem for pastors. There are a host of problems we could choose. We will, however, focus on the problem of money because most pastors see money as the part of their job that takes them farthest from their calling as ministers of the gospel. Many report it is their most frustrating problem. They lament that dealing with money reduces them to "a company of shopkeepers" hawking their wares.[1] The worst meeting of the year is when the board debates the budget. And the most awkward sermons come at stewardship time. Pastors report that money questions uproot them from their calling to preach, teach, and counsel, instead entangling them in the administrative issues that they find least satisfying. Money creates problems for pastors.[2]

How do the lessons of this book apply to the money question? The central argument has been that pastors can use the preaching and teaching gifts that come most naturally to them to do the organizational work of leadership that often seems unnatural to them.[3] If that argument works, then pastors need a richer vocabulary and an understanding of theological categories and not just organizational skills. In other words, we should be able to reframe the money question so that it is primarily an interpretative question rather than an administrative one.

The most powerful sermons, as we learned in the introduction, are the ones that provide a spiritual interpretation for the things that keep people awake at night. When people think about the things that are closest to their hearts, we want them to use Christian categories. And money is certainly one of the things that keep people awake at night with worry. So it would follow that pastors should have a trove of sermons on money. But that is not the case.

Pastors can use the preaching and teaching gifts that come most naturally to them to do the organizational work of leadership that often seems unnatural to them.

Many pastors have learned only three sermons when it comes to money. And each sermon is wrong. There is the pat-the-poor-on-the-head sermon that encourages those who worry about money to "consider the lilies of the field" and dismisses the problem because "the poor will always be with you." There is the buying-things-is-wrong sermon that describes money "as the root of all evil" and condemns people for their crass materialism. And there is, of course, the give-me-your-money-so-you-can-stop-feeling-guilty sermon. As I said, each one is wrong. But each one also contains a kernel of truth. Jesus did say that we should think about the ways that God clothed the lilies. First Timothy (and common sense) does testify that "the love of money is a root of all kinds of evil" (6:10). And God does call us to give generously. Each of these distorted sermons contains a kernel of truth.

The problem is not just that these sermons are distorted. The problem is that these are the only interpretations many American pastors have when discussing money, possessions, and work. As Robert Wuthnow discovered when he asked pastors about these questions, clergy long for a richer language.[4] They want to be able to do justice to the complicated situations that their parishioners live with each day. And they want to be able to speak to the anxieties that their people ponder when they lie awake at night.

That is where the lessons from this book become important. Part 1 developed eight guidelines for framing an issue theologically. The next section of this conclusion will describe how each of the eight guidelines illumines a Christian view of money. Then the final section will show how to apply the guidelines to interpret three aspects of the money problem.

1. Change people's expectations

If you ask parishioners what they expect the church to say about money, the answers are not surprising. People expect the church to ask for money—either for the church's own purposes or for the sake of the needy.[5] People do not expect the church to understand that they have legitimate worries about money. And they certainly do not expect that the church can be a place that they can talk honestly to each other and to God about their worries.

So the first item on our agenda is to change the way that we as ministers discuss money. When a family is worried about affording health insurance, or sending kids to college, or providing care for aging parents, these are legitimate worries. They are not the product of indulgent materialism. They come from an appropriate desire to care for loved ones. But in the present church context, those concerns rarely make it into our discussions of money. Why not? Because the mental models we use—the three standard sermons—do not provide a place to consider monetary worries that are legitimate. So we need to . . .

2. Draw from a different repertoire

There are at least three ways to reframe a Christian view of money that do not draw on the repertoire of the standard, outmoded sermons that usually get preached on the topic. They are (a) tell people that God wants their honesty, even and especially if they are angry with God, (b) give people language for discussing their work life either as a curse or as a blessing, and (c) shift the conversation about giving so that the discussion moves away from duty and toward generosity.

The first allows ministers to address the question of the legitimate money concerns that keep people awake at night with worry. Many people cannot talk honestly about money because they are angry, and they mistakenly believe that it is blasphemous to be angry in church or at God. Others think that worrying shows a lack of faith. So they hide their fears from the church. If people are going to rethink their concerns, however, they have to be able to talk about them without fear of condemnation by the church. When people believe that they will be blamed for their fears, it is unlikely that they will speak honestly about them. So the first thing that a minister can do to reframe the money question is to draw from a repertoire that allows honesty without fear. A minister might start, for example, by preaching from Romans 8:1, which says, "there is no con-demnation for those who are in Christ Jesus." Such a pericope would allow the preacher to tell stories about people who worry about money. Then the preacher might conclude by saying that God will not condemn us simply for worrying. The tagline might be, "God does not blame us for our fears." This naturally leads to the question of what is an appropriate way to bring our fears to God, even and especially when we are angry with God. That would be the time to discuss the biblical form of the lament.

The lament is the most common type of psalm. These psalms of lament, however, are not the ones we usually read aloud in church. They are the ones that describe the psalmist's troubles and ask God to do some-thing about it. And sometimes they can express anger directly at God. If we had to vote today on psalms, most of these laments would not make it into the canon because they do not fit what we think Scripture should be. But there they are, as models for people to pray when they are in trouble. We can thus use these psalms as models for parishioners who have fears about money. We can say, "God wants your honesty. In fact, God pro-vided a bunch of psalms as models so that you will know it is okay to speak honestly and directly to God—even and especially when you are angry." The first new repertoire allows our people to bring their fears hon-estly before God.

The second way that we can draw interpretations from a new repertoire involves giving parishioners fresh language for describing their work life. Most of our congregants spend the majority of the week at a job. Yet we have not given them language for discussing that job from a Christian perspective. And indeed, there will be different interpretations for differ-ent experiences of work. Some people hate the work that they do. Others love it. Most experiences are somewhere in between.

The Bible reflects both perspectives. It describes labor as a curse that comes as a result of human sinfulness. And it describes what theologians call the idea of "vocation" or "calling" from God. A pastor who wishes to reframe the conversation about money will need to introduce language to describe labor. And that language will have to reflect both the negative and the positive experiences people have in working.

The third way that we can reinterpret how parishioners view money is to change the way we describe the act of giving. Every church service has a moment when people are invited to give money. The typical way that people interpret this moment is as a necessary evil. The logic goes something like this: we have to pay our pastor and our electric bill, which means that we have to have money, which means that congregants have to give it. Thus the offering becomes something like the price of admission.

One way to reinterpret the act of giving is to focus on cultivating generosity. The purpose of the church is not simply to stay open. The purpose of the church is to enable people to become more like Christ. And Christ was generous, not selfish. The current logic of give-to-pay-the-pastor can feel self-serving to congregants. But cultivating generosity is a good thing. No one is going to question that the church can and should be doing that. So we may want to draw from the language of generosity rather than portraying giving as a duty that is necessary to keep the lights on.

3. Use a narrative structure

People think in terms of stories. That is how they arrange the information that comes to them. So one of the most effective ways to get people to rethink Christianity and money is to provide a standard narrative for arranging that information. Within each of the three outmoded sermons that preachers presently use, there is an embedded narrative. Within the "lilies-of-the-field" sermon is a story that says that there is nothing for the church to do for the poor. The end of the story dominates everything else in it. And the result is the feeling that there is no reason to bring money issues to the church. Within the "materialism-is-bad" sermon is a morality play that casts anyone who purchases stuff as a materialist. So the moral of every person's story is the same, according to this sermon: you would not have these worries if you would just stop buying things. And, finally, the "give-to-the-church" sermon asks people to step into a story about duty. The answer to every question is that you have a duty to give. In each case, the end point or the lesson one draws from the story determines the usefulness of the story. The lesson from the first story is that the poor should worry less. The lesson of the second is to stop buying things. And the lesson of the third is to give what you have to the church. The combination of the three stories says, "Quit complaining, stop buying stuff, and give your money to the church." Now, I don't know any pastor who would preach that in a sermon. It is too extreme. Yet the stories embedded in our current sermons on money end up with people hearing just that sort of message.[6]

It then becomes important for us to construct alternative story lines and to invite people to step into them. How, for example, might we create an alternative to the idea—embedded in the "lilies-of-the-field" sermon—that worrying is wrong? The best way to do that is to offer a different model for someone who felt great worry and then to invite people to follow that person's example. The most compelling example of such a person is Jesus, who prayed with such anxiety in the garden of Gethsemane that he asked the disciples to wait with him because he was so troubled (Matthew 26) and who cried out in sorrow to God from the cross. How did Jesus handle his anxiety? He brought it directly to God and he did it in the company of other believers. The story of Jesus in Gethsemane or Jesus crying out from the cross can provide an antidote to those who say that good Christians should not worry about the future.

Another way to use a narrative structure is to provide an example of someone who once held to one view and then adopted a new view. For example, I know a story about a woman who thought that Ephesians 4 commanded her never to worry about anything. And thus she believed that all worry was sinful. I could tell that story and then show how she learned a new way of interpreting that verse to be an admonition to pray and not a prohibition of worry. Any new interpretation of money will have to include narratives that allow people to reinterpret their experiences.

4. Create a clear set of actions

This is the logical next step from the stories we tell. The implication of talking about Jesus in the garden of Gethsemane is to say that, "You should be like Jesus. When he was worried about the future, he did two things. He prayed. And he asked other believers to pray with him. You should do the same." Or, if I were to tell the story about misinterpreting Ephesians, I would say, "The lesson of the passage is not what this woman thought it was. She thought it said, 'Don't worry.' But instead it said, 'When you worry, pray.' And that's what you should do, pray." The goal is not only to tell a story. The goal is to tell a story that has a clear set of actions attached to it.

5. Tap into pre-legitimated pathways

One important way to get access to fresh interpretations is to look for new ways of applying concepts that are already in circulation. We have already alluded to an idea that only works because it comes pre-legitimated: that is, the psalms of lament as models for speaking honestly with God.

The lament, as we have mentioned, is the most prevalent form in the Psalms. Many of the psalms cry out to God from the midst of distress, and they implicate God. "O God, why do you cast us off forever? / Why does your anger smoke against the sheep of your pasture?" (Psalm 74:1). "Is the enemy to revile your name forever? / Why do you hold back your hand?" (Psalm 74:10-11). The implication is that the trouble that surrounds the psalmist would disappear if God would only act. This is not the way we are accustomed to praying. We have learned to speak reverently and not to question God. But the psalmist brings raw anger and fear directly to God—and does so without sinning.

Most parishioners would think that showing such ire toward God would be blasphemous. But here it is in the Psalms, written down in the prayer book for God's people. It would seem illegitimate to most parishioners if the pastor stood up and said to be honest with God even if you are angry. We believe God deserves respect. And that respect would preclude us from speaking "disrespectfully" to God. Yet the Psalms come pre-legitimated. No pastor has to convince a congregation that a psalm provides an appropriate model for prayer. Thus, by tapping into the Psalms' legitimacy, the pastor can convince people to speak in a way that they would never consider if the model were not present in the Bible. The legitimacy of the Psalms makes the lesson possible.

6. Legitimate fresh interpretations

Sometimes, however, it becomes necessary to introduce people to an interpretation that they may not have heard before. For example, we earlier said that one way to understand work is as a calling. Many parishioners will have heard ministers refer to their work as a calling. But most have not heard anyone describe secular labor that way. In such a moment, one option is to explain to people about the theological concept of vocation—that each Christian is called by God to do something to contribute to God's work in the world. For some people, that work indeed is a full-time religious occupation. But for others it is no occupation at all. Sunday school teachers, for example, fit this description. And still others may be called by God to work outside the church in what is, nevertheless, a calling. Nurses, or others in the helping professions, might feel called of God and describe their work as a vocation. Perhaps musicians and artists might describe the creative work that they do as a vocation. There are even accountants and businessmen and businesswomen who feel called by God to do the labor that they do. The idea of vocation says that each person is called of God to some kind of redemptive labor. But most people do not know about this theological concept. So it becomes the minister's role to explain that idea to people so that they can seek out work that they can describe as a calling.

7. The goal is to internalize

The biggest organizational advantage that a minister has, compared to leaders in other settings, is the opportunity to preach each week. Those twenty minutes a week are crucial because the pastor can use them to repeat certain themes and reinforce new ideas until people make them their own. That means, however, that a pastor cannot preach about money only during a stewardship drive. Indeed, I would think that preachers would find it least effective to preach about money at exactly the point when people are expecting to hear one of the three outmoded sermons. If a minister preaches on money during October, it would be easy for people who expect a "give-me-your-money" sermon to recast whatever the preacher says into a plea for funds, even if the pastor meant nothing of the sort. It would be far more effective to preach about money at other times of the year and to weave money themes into other sermons. For example, during Lent many pastors preach on Jesus in the garden of Gethsemane pleading with God. That would be a good time to talk about the things that worry our parishioners and to help those anxious congregants to follow Jesus' example by speaking honestly to God about their fears. In fact, the best way to encourage people to internalize an idea is to find a phrase that summarizes that idea and to reference it in many different sermons. For example, on money, one might want to draw on phrases like "God cares about the things we hold most dear," or "God invites our honesty, even and especially when we are angry at God," or, as we will see below, "generosity is the antidote to selfishness." Any of these phrases is versatile enough to work in a number of sermons. The goal is to get the congregation to pick up the phrase and to start using it for themselves. When they do that, they have internalized the idea and made it their own.

8. We cannot control the meaning people make

When Jesus preached in the synagogues around Capernaum and healed the sick, it should have been obvious that he was the Messiah. Or so we think from our perspective. But at the time, the Pharisees saw him, not as a messenger from God, but as a blasphemer who would distort the Law to which they had dedicated their lives. And even his most trusted followers were not sure what meaning to make of his message. John the Baptist sent word in Luke 7, asking if Jesus were the Anointed One. Jesus healed the sick, preached with an unprecedented authority, forgave sins, and even raised the dead. Yet he found that there were many answers to the question, "Who do people say that I am?" (Mark 8:27). Even Jesus could not control the meaning people make.

That means, of course, that no preacher can control meaning making either. People will sometimes hear something very different from what the pastor intended.

Leaders can shape meaning but they cannot dictate it.

So it becomes important to monitor what people are hearing. Ask people, for example, about their ideas regarding money. Listen to the vocabulary people use in their answers. Listen for the categories that you have been preaching about. And see if they mean the same thing that you meant when you used the words. It is easy for a preacher to assume that people hear what the preacher meant to say. But that is rarely the case. It is important to remember that leaders can *shape* meaning but they cannot *dictate* it.

These are the eight guidelines developed earlier in the book. As you can see, each one relates in some ways to the question of Christianity and money. But how do they all come together? For the last portion of this conclusion, I give examples of how to combine the lessons learned above into a new perspective on money.

The best way to discuss money may be to break the question into three parts. The first part deals with the monetary pressures that many people feel in everyday life. The second discusses ways to help people understand their work in godly terms. And the final part seeks a better way to interpret the act of giving. Together they should provide a new repertoire of sermons for pastors who wish to reinterpret the issue of money for their congregations.

Monetary Pressures

The most important place to begin any Christian discussion of money, I believe, is by acknowledging the real and legitimate anxieties that people feel about money. In the Introduction, we talked about the *Time* magazine article that described contemporary concerns. "This is not just crass materialism," the article said. "Many of the new musts are not goods but services—medical insurance, day care for young children, college tuition for teenagers—that have rocketed in price."[7] When people lie awake at night worrying about caring for their elderly parents or about how to pay for prescription drugs, the rhetoric of selfish materialism does not apply. These are legitimate worries. But what happens when the very idea of worry becomes controversial?

Not long ago, I was working with the Board of Elders at a local church in Northern California. It was an interesting mix of wise senior citizens and energetic young adults. They were particularly interested in how to think about money. I told them that congregations need to address the concerns that keep people awake at night. Most of the people in the room nodded; that made sense to them. But one of the women began to scowl. From earlier conversations, I knew she was the most spiritually respected person in the room—kind of a Protestant nun. She was not pleased. So I asked her what was on her mind. She answered by quoting Scripture. "Do not be anxious about anything," she said quoting chapter 4 of the Apostle Paul's letter to the Philippians, "but in everything, by prayer and petition, with thanksgiving, present your requests to God." After a little more conversation, she came to her conclusion. "It is a sin to worry. And we shouldn't encourage it by indulging people's fears."

"It is a sin to worry," she said. That is the first obstacle to honest talk about faith and money. This deeply pious and well-respected church leader was saying, in effect, that any person who admitted that they sometimes lay awake at night worrying about money should admit to it with the same attitude that they used when they confessed any other sin. And it is hard to begin a conversation that way. But I believe that her premise needs to be examined. Is it really a sin to worry? Do we have examples of faithful people who were deeply troubled by something? Sure, Moses, David, Peter, and Paul leap to mind. But they were mere mortals. Each one is also famous for some spectacular sin. So we can't conclude anything about worrying being sin simply by observing their behavior. Ah, but what about Jesus? In the garden of Gethsemane, he poured out his soul to God and told the disciples, "my heart is deeply troubled." Surely, he was anxious for something in that moment. And none of us are prepared to call that sin. So perhaps we can take "Be anxious for nothing" to be an encouragement to pray rather than a prohibition of worry. But that just begs a new question. How should we pray when we are worried?

This is where we can learn from Scripture. In the days when the people of Israel were wandering in the wilderness between Egypt and Canaan, they were not always happy with Moses (or God). Indeed, they often engaged in a behavior that the Old Testament calls "grumbling." For example, Numbers 14 opens this way, "All the Israelites grumbled against Moses and Aaron, and the whole assembly said to them, 'If only we had died in Egypt! Or in this desert! Why is the LORD bringing us to this land only to let us fall by the sword? Our wives and children will be taken as plunder. Wouldn't it be better for us to go back to Egypt?' And they said to each other, 'We should choose a leader and go back to Egypt'" (vv. 2-4 NIV). By the middle of the chapter, however, Yahweh has pronounced judgment on them, saying that those who grumbled against God and against Moses would be punished. They would be destined to wander in the desert without ever entering the land that God would give to their descendents. Another way to translate this word *grumble* is call it a complaint—a complaint that brings God's sure punishment. Worry may not be a sin, but it appears that complaining is.[8]

What's the difference? The answer gets more confusing before it becomes clear. Look again at the psalms of lament. They are the ones that cry out in pain—and often implicate God in allowing their pain to continue. Earlier, we looked at Psalm 74. Let's turn now to Psalm 22, which begins, "My God, my God, why have you forsaken me? / Why are you so far from helping me, from the words of my groaning? / O my God, I cry by day, but you do not answer; / and by night, but find no rest" (vv. 1-2). It goes on to express trust in God but to continue the lamenting tone that questions God. The lament is a legitimate way to express anxiety and even anger toward God. The reason the Hebrew Psalter is filled with these laments is so that God's people will have language for being honest before God—a well-worn pathway to heart-wrenching honesty. And what is the other word that scholars use when talking about a lament? They call it a complaint.[9]

So we have an interesting dilemma. Some complaints (the grumbling kind) deserve judgment. Other complaints (the lamenting kind) are models for honest prayers before God. The distinctions between grumbling and lament will give us the first insight we need when talking about money. I believe the distinction has to do with trust. The Psalms make it perfectly clear that God wants us to be utterly honest—even and especially when we are angry at God or worried about what we lack. But in Numbers 14, the people of God take that anger too far. They claim that God (and Moses) can no longer be trusted. This was the same people who witnessed with their own eyes the dramatic way that God intervened to rescue them when Pharaoh's chariots bore down on them on the shores of the Red Sea. And they were so worried that they had lost faith in God. They no longer believed that God could be trusted. Psalm 22, on the other hand, begins as we have seen with a direct indictment of God, "Why are you so far from helping me?" But it goes on to express a confident hope that someday "the poor shall eat and be satisfied" and "those who seek him shall praise the LORD" (v. 26). The difference between a lament and grumbling is that a lament contains a clear statement of trust.

How might one use such a lament when burdened with worry? Look to Jesus' example. What did he cry out in his moment of greatest anguish? "My God, My God, why have you forsaken me?" And where does that come from? The first line of Psalm 22, "My God, My God, why have you forsaken me? / Why are you so far from helping me . . . ?" Jesus was quoting the first line of a psalm of lament. It is like quoting the first line of a song. When we say, "My country 'tis of thee," the phrase itself makes no sense on its own. "My country, it is of you"; what does that mean? It means nothing on its own. But it is a placeholder for

> The difference between the lament and grumbling is that the lament continues to express trust in God, while grumbling chooses to abandon that trust.

the whole song. "My country it is of you I sing." And in the same way that the opening of the song implies everything that the song implies, so Jesus' use of the lament while dying on the cross was a way to imply all that the lament meant. He could cry out in anguish because (as Psalm 22:16 KJV says) "they pierced my hands and my feet." But he did it in such a way that his anguish never destroyed his trust. He continued to believe that, in the words of verse 24, God "heard when [the afflicted] cried to him." The difference between the lament and grumbling is that the lament continues to express trust in God, while grumbling chooses to abandon that trust.

How does this relate to Christianity and money? In my experience, one of the reasons that church people do not talk about their fears honestly in church is that they are worried that they will be blamed for their fears. So one of the things we who lead God's people can do is resurrect an old category—the lament. We can change their expectations. Many Christians believe that their worries betray a lack of faith. So they hide their fears and we in the church cannot talk honestly about the things that matter most to us. By reintroducing the language of lament, we can begin to convince people that God wants to hear their honest complaints. Indeed, God is so interested in listening to their fears that God provides many examples in the Psalms of just how to speak openly and with anguished honesty directly to God. If we somehow had to ratify these psalms nowadays, they would never make it into the Psalter because people would see them as disrespectful or even blasphemous. But they are there. And they are there for a reason. They are there to remind us that God welcomes our worries, and even our anger. If we are going to take people's legitimate worries about money seriously, we must begin by giving them a language for taking those worries directly to God.

We have another obligation as well. It is easy for people to get so caught up in their own anxieties that they do not see the blessings all around them. So we have an obligation not only to give them a language for lament but also to instill in them a habit of gratitude. Almost every person who reads this book is blessed with a level of prosperity that makes each of us incredibly wealthy by global standards. Many people in the world live on two dollars a day, which is approximately what I spent this morning on coffee. We are wealthy and we are blessed. And such blessing should inspire gratitude in the people of God. I have been quite moved, for example, by reading Walter Brueggemann's article entitled, "The Liturgy of Abundance, the Myth of Scarcity."[10] We are tempted to make scarcity the primary lens we use to interpret the world. Yet so much of the Scripture celebrates God's rich blessing. We live in a world of abundance. That is the message of the psalms that celebrate creation (e.g., Psalm 19) and that is the message of Jesus' admonition to "consider the lilies of the field." God provides—and we who live in the lap of American luxury can never forget that.

Notice the order in which these ideas are presented, however. We need to provide people the language of lament so they can express their anxieties before we can remind them that God has provided for them a world of abundance. We will indeed ask people to eventually shift their mental models from scarcity to abundance. But we have to do it at a pace they can stand. And people who do not feel that the church has heard the legitimate fears that keep them awake at night will never give us the authority to tell them that they live in a world of abundance rather than scarcity. Gratitude can thus only come once people have had a chance to express their lament.

> We need to provide people the language of lament so they can express their anxieties before we can remind them that God has provided for them a world of abundance.

Work Life

If the first step toward making spiritual meaning about money is to provide a language for being honest with God and with each other about the financial pressures each of us feels, the second step is to make some sense of work. Most adults spend their days working. Some folks get paid for it; others (such as stay-at-home moms or full-time students) do not. Either way, most of us spend the typical weekday doing labor. This labor is a crucial part of what it means to be an adult in our society. It takes a significant amount of our time and tends to shape the way that we see ourselves. We say things like, "I am a nurse" or "My father was an engineer." It goes to our very sense of self.[11]

How then are we to understand in Christian terms this concept of work? There have been many answers over the centuries of Christian history. But I want to focus on two: labor as a curse, and vocation as a blessing.

Most theological discussions of labor begin in the garden of Eden. It is part of the *Imago Dei*. We labor because we are made in the image of the God who created and sustains the universe. Some emphasize that, even before the Fall, Adam and Eve had work to do. They were asked to name the animals, for example. God also gave them a mandate before they left the garden—a mandate to have dominion on the earth. There are thus some theologians who emphasize that honest labor is a good thing. It is a blessing to the worker and to the world. And, as such, is something that we should celebrate. There are those, however, who emphasize something else that happened in the garden. After the Fall, God cursed humanity, saying "By the sweat of your brow, you will eat food." From this verse, many have come to the conclusion that work has now become a curse. They remind us that it takes hard work (and not just honest labor) to coax the ground to produce a crop and that there will always be parts of every job that are drudgery. Work they conclude is now a curse. So there are two sides to the debate. One says that honest labor is a blessing. And the other says that hard work is a curse.[12]

I would like to argue that each of these perspectives contains truth and each one misses something crucial. At some point, each of us experiences our work as drudgery. But it goes further than that. There are some jobs that, by their very nature, are mind numbing or physically destructive. If you are Employee #432 in a factory and your job is to insert Widget #18b onto Assembly #76, there is not much in your job that can fulfill you. For eight hours each day, you do one thing. It never calls for your best efforts or inspires you to be more than you were the day they hired you. There is none of the craftsman's satisfaction in seeing the finished product. Workers in such a position often report that they end up feeling less than human, no better than a robot designed solely for inserting widgets. This dehumanizing quality of some work is indeed tragic. But I am not sure that it is fair to blame God for it. Calling this a curse that results from the Fall strikes me as blaming God for something that derives instead from sinful human systems.[13]

There are, however, some jobs that are physically destructive. Citrus trees and strawberry fields surround the town where I was raised. It is not uncommon to see laborers stooped over the strawberry plants, toiling in the sun. This backbreaking labor is destructive to the people who have to do it. The presence of these people reminds us how dangerous it is to succumb to the temptation to think of labor as another word for someone's career. We can too easily picture an air-conditioned office with a water cooler next to the copy machine whenever we talk about work. Some people do indeed experience labor as a curse—as a destructive necessity.[14]

So we find that not only do we have to acknowledge that people have legitimate anxieties about money, we also have to give people the language to express their pain over having to toil in order to live. If we do not give people the opportunity and the vocabulary to express their pain, any attempts we later make to encourage them to change their behavior will ring hollow. Until we understand people's fears and their pain—and until they understand that we understand—we will not have the right to ask people to change. We have to provide a language for expressing anger, fear, and pain before we can move on to discuss other aspects of the spiritual meaning of money.

> Until we understand people's fears and their pain we will not have the right to ask people to change.

There is, however, another language that needs to sit side by side with this language of pain. When we discuss work, we also have to introduce the idea of vocation. If backbreaking labor is less than a career, vocation involves an understanding of work that goes beyond the idea of a career. A vocation is a calling from God. Let me give an example to illustrate what I mean.

When I was a college student, I majored in Computer Engineering. I expected that when I graduated from college, I would take a job as a computer programmer. But God intervened. I eventually became convinced that God was calling me to some kind of ministry. It happened, oddly enough, because of a preacher's aside. The preacher was discussing the first part of Ephesians, discussing how God had "lavished" good things upon us. He was describing a study he had made of the Greek word for "lavish" when he paused. He left his lesson for a moment to marvel at the privilege he felt at being able to spend all day, each day serving God and studying Scripture. And then he returned to his lesson. But I did not hear that rest of what he said. In that aside, God spoke to me. After the service, I went off to pray—because I knew something was happening. I felt God telling me that I would "devote my professional life to serving God."

I knew that God was telling me that I would spend my workdays in direct Christian service. I had a hard time, at first, explaining to people the feeling that this call created in me. I felt it was both a privilege and a compulsion. On the one hand, I was honored and pleased to be able to do what I loved to do. On the other hand, I found it daunting. At the same time that I felt the privilege, I felt the weight. I knew that to do anything else was to be disobedient. And that made me uncomfortable. I wanted to choose my career and not to have anyone else tell me what to do. Eventually I came to realize that the privilege and the compulsion came together. It was a promise that I would not have a mere career; I would have a calling. But it was a compulsion because I knew that, once God called, I had no choice but to follow.

The irony is that I thought I understood exactly what that calling meant. I enrolled in seminary expecting to be a minister or a missionary—because I had looked around and decided that was what God needed. What I did not consider was my own giftedness. It turned out I would be a lousy missionary and, probably, a mediocre pastor. That is not where my giftedness lies. Fortunately, God was not finished with me. Halfway through seminary I realized that I could either be a professorial pastor or a pastoral professor. So I went to graduate school and got a job teaching in a seminary. But that's the point; it was not just a job. I have experienced my work as a vocation. I am doing just what God has called me to do.

The danger, however, is to think that these ideas of calling and vocation apply only to ministry. In the same way that God has called me to be a professor, God could easily have called me to some other kind of work— even as a computer engineer. The important distinction is not between Christian work and secular labor. The important question is this. Are you doing what God has called you to do? And is that labor an extension of the giftedness God has planted within you? My mother, for example, spent many years as a nurse. She described it as a calling from God. It required her to use the giftedness that God had given her and it provided for her a venue for ministering to others in God's name. Likewise, I know women who describe mothering as their calling.

If God has led a person to a particular labor and if that labor allows a person to express the Spirit that God has planted in them, then they are exercising a vocation. This vocation is a privilege and a compulsion. It is a response to God's calling. It is a privilege to be called by the Most High

God, but mere mortals have no business refusing the gifts that God lavishes on those whom God calls.[15]

So, to summarize, we have to acknowledge that we experience labor as both a curse and as a blessing. And it is in the tension between the two that we live. We cannot deny either without distorting what it means to be human. Thus any notion of Christianity and money must include these complementary and competitive ideas.

This understanding of work, however, is not yet complete. It fails to address the idea of Sabbath. Any explanation of labor must include God's clear plan that all labor cease for one day in seven. When God labored to create the world, God rested on the Sabbath. When God led the Hebrews in wandering through the wilderness and when God provided manna to feed those Hebrews, God rested one day in seven. And when God defined the laws that were to guide the life of God's people, it included a commandment to "Remember the Sabbath day and keep it holy."

This rhythm of labor and rest appears in other places as well. Crops were to lay fallow after a period of years. And debts were to be forgiven in the Jubilee year. The important lesson is that there is more to life than labor—even labor that is a vocation. This Sabbath lesson is important in contemporary congregations because many of our parishioners find that they have more money than time. Time is the precious commodity that they horde. They feel compelled to activity—either from external necessity or internal compunction. In such circumstances, they need to hear God's command to rest. Just as humans work because God works, in the same way, we rest because God rested.

> Just as humans work because God works, in the same way, we rest because God rested.

Giving

The first step in discussing Christianity and money was to provide a language for being honest with God about our fears. The second step was to acknowledge that work is both a curse and a blessing. Only when that language is firmly established are we ready to discuss giving. The first two steps allow people to describe their experiences in spiritual terms. Neither of the steps, however, is predominately about changing people's behavior. Instead, they are designed to reframe their experience so that they can see that experience in spiritual terms. This last step, on the other hand, does require people to change.[16]

There are many motivations that preachers use when they attempt to motivate people to give. Some talk about the good things that the money will buy—whether food for the hungry or electricity to light the sanctuary. Others talk about God's commandments and make giving a matter of obedience. This is the biblical equivalent to the parent who says, "Because I said so." And, then, there are preachers who emphasize the urgency of some crisis. "If you don't give, we will have to close the project." I disagree with each of these rationales. Talk of utility (i.e., give to accomplish something) turns givers into consumers who purchase services. The problem here is that, in a world where the customer is always right, people begin to think of themselves as having control over which things get done. Almost every pastor has met the parishioner who threatens to take their money elsewhere if they don't get their way. A congregation's primary responsibility is to serve God and not to be swayed from doing good by the giver who wants to have their way. Likewise, the call to obedience is not the best way to inspire giving because it is too easy for the preacher to become the voice of God—that is, it's too easy for the message to shift away from obedience to God and toward obedience to the minister. Don't get me wrong. I do believe that Christians should give because God commands it. But I also believe that the pastor who preaches such obedience as the primary motivation for giving runs the risk of claiming God's authority for himself. And, finally, the crisis appeal plays off what I believe is a distortion of God's provision. It emphasizes what one scholar has called "the myth of scarcity" rather than celebrating the God of abundance. In other words, if we continually emphasize scarcity we run the risk of leading our people to believe that they (and not God) are the ones who provide.[17]

I am not saying that it is always inappropriate to use these three rationales for giving. I have used each one and will no doubt use each again. Instead I am saying that they need to be used sparingly and thus cannot serve as the primary reason that we use when we call on people to give. What then is the best reason for people to give?[18] I would offer three motivations in their place.

First, we should each give because generosity is a good thing. It is the opposite of selfishness. It does not take a deep theological analysis to convince a congregation that selfishness is at the root of all kinds of evil. All they have to do is look around them—or to take a look at their own lives. Selfishness is one of the first negative behaviors we see in toddlers. It is one of the most difficult attitudes to root out in teens. And it remains prevalent in the adults most of us encounter each day. Selfishness in its various forms is rampant. Generosity is the antidote to selfishness. We sometimes think that the opposite of some sinful behavior is the absence of that behavior. But I would argue that the opposite of selfishness is not the absence of selfishness. The opposite is to do good—to practice generosity. A pastor can ask people to give because giving makes the giver a better person.[19]

The second reason to give is that we each bear a responsibility for one another. I believe that we often create a free agent model of Christianity, especially when we talk about giving. The logic of our preaching often says that each individual makes her own decision apart from the community of faith. We certainly don't talk about how much we give. In fact, that would be considered rude in most congregations. Yet, if we are indeed a *community* of faith, then we each bear a responsibility for one another. I am specifically not interested in having someone stand up in church and tell other people that they have to start giving their fair share. That's like the kid who saw a woman with a soda and said, "Let's share. Me first." It turns a gift into a demand. And that does not help anyone. If, on the other hand, a pastor can help a person see that he bears a responsibility to his neighbor, then that provides one more rationale for giving.

Finally, there is a time and a place for talking about sacrifice. I hesitate to bring this up because the notion of "sacrificial giving" has been abused by generations of pastors. When I talk about sacrifice with a congregation, however, I start small. I want them to think about some small way that they can give up something. For example, my wife and I were talking with our children about how much we should give to various causes. At the end of the discussion we came to the question of how much we should donate to help two young ladies in our church go to work for a summer in a Kenyan AIDS orphanage. We agreed on an amount. But my daughter did not think it was enough. So we asked her what she would be willing to give up in order for us to give more. She did not understand at first. So we explained the concept of sacrifice. In the end, she agreed to give up our monthly visit to her favorite restaurant so that we could increase what we gave to these women. It was not a big sacrifice in that it only netted a few more dollars. But it was, for my daughter, the next faithful step. And that was far more important than the money. It made her more generous and it fought against the corrosive effects of selfishness. Sacrifice is an important category for people to have when they think about money.

There are many more things one could say about Christianity and money. But our purpose here was not to give a definitive treatment so much as it was to provide a model for practicing some of the ideas that we have discussed in this book. In this last section, let me revisit this discussion of money to show how we used ideas that were developed earlier in the book.

The first and most important task is to change people's expectations. People expect preachers to preach self-interested sermons about money— sermons designed to get the preachers more money. So we must defeat that stereotype by listening well to the anxieties that money brings out for people. But it goes further than that. We need to provide them with the language—the theological categories—to describe how to make spiritual sense of money and of the issues that it creates in their lives.

We provide new cultural resources by introducing biblical concepts like the lament. This gives them a different repertoire from which to draw when they construct their interpretations. People have expected that God (and God's church) could not handle their anger or their fears. They believe it would be irreverent to speak honestly to God. By drawing their attention to the laments, they get examples of how faithful Hebrews spoke directly to God.

These laments also illustrate the insight that a clear set of actions should follow from our interpretations. What are faithful Christians to do when they find themselves beset by worry? Do the same thing Jesus did on the cross. Pray a psalm of lament. Jesus chose Psalm 22, "My God, my God, why have you forsaken me?" This is one of many psalms that combine honest questioning with sincere trust. The psalms of lament provide not only a language for speaking honestly to God about our fears, but they also provide a clear set of actions. Pray this way when you feel angry with God.

And, finally, there is an alternate story that holds all these together. The old story is that God cannot handle your anger. The new story is that

God welcomes your honesty and indeed provides you with biblical models for how to speak honestly. The very trajectory of the story shifts from moving away from God to moving toward God.

That is what it means to make spiritual meaning. It means creating a Christian way of seeing the world that enables and encourages people to take new action. It means providing vocabulary and theological categories. It means pointing people toward new theological interpretations, new ways of framing their values, and new goals. And it means weaving new stories that hold all these cultural resources together. In the end, leaders who make spiritual meaning invite their congregations to live in a new interpretative world.

Notes

1. Eugene Peterson, *Working the Angles: The Shape of Pastoral Integrity*, 1 (see part 2, n. 3).

2. Daniel Conway, Anita Rook, and Daniel A. Schipp, *The Reluctant Steward: A Report and Commentary on The Stewardship and Development Study* (Indianapolis, Ind. and St. Meinrad, Ind.: Christian Theological Seminary and Saint Meinrad Seminary, 1992).

3. Please note that I am not saying that preaching is a substitute for administration. I am saying that preachers can use their interpretive gifts to help with administrative tasks.

4. Wuthnow, *The Crisis in the Churches*, see especially pp. 5–9 on the need for spiritual interpretation and pp. 71–86 for the words that the clergy use to describe their dilemma.

5. Wuthnow, *The Crisis in the Churches*, esp. pp. 54–86.

6. Perhaps the most painfully telling support for this point is to look to comedy. Comedy works because it places our subtle messages in bold type. And one of the most prevalent ways that preachers are skewered by satire is to portray them as money-hungry and insensitive to the poor.

7. Church, "Are We Better Off?" *Time* (see intro, n. 7).

8. My thinking in this section has been strongly influenced by Walter Brueggemann, especially the collection of articles published in *Deep Memory, Exuberant Hope: Contested Truth in a Post-Christian World* (Minneapolis: Fortress Press, 2000).

9. On the psalms of lament, see especially Patrick D. Miller, *They Cried to the Lord: The Form and Theology of Biblical Prayer* (Minneapolis: Fortress Press, 1994).

10. Brueggemann, "The Liturgy of Abundance, the Myth of Scarcity" in *Deep Memory, Exuberant Hope*, 69–76.

11. Our current social configuration also shapes our very notion of labor. It is hard for me to write without thinking of the abstract concepts of work and labor as being synonymous with the more particular notion of one's job. The idea of labor—especially when it comes to theological discussions—must however extend beyond one's job. For example, it takes work to make a meal. Things are not simply handed to us. We have to work in order

to get the basic necessities of food and shelter. In the garden of Eden, it is not clear that these daily labors were necessary. God simply provided for Adam and Eve.

12. The best summary of the theological issues related to questions of work is Miroslav Volf, *The Work of the Spirit: Toward a Theology of Work* (Eugene, Ore.: Wipf and Stock, 2001).

13. I do indeed believe that human systems can be destructive and thus sinful. These systems are such that no one person in the system is responsible for the destruction that the systems cause. But each person in the system contributes to the destructive whole.

14. Other people find the need to work as another kind of destructive necessity. I am thinking, for example, of single parents who have to leave their children for long periods of time each day in order to earn enough for the family to live. These parents know that their children would be better off if the parents did not have to leave them. But they know that going off to work is the only way to feed and clothe their children. Thus they feel that the need to work is destructive.

15. I should acknowledge that there is a temptation to see the Christian idea of vocation in profoundly individualistic terms. There are at least two areas where this happens. First, we forget that the community of faith must confirm any calling from God—and that the voice of God often comes through the community of faith. Second, we forget that any labor we do as Christians must always be seen as an extension of the work of God's people. None of us acts alone. We are representatives of God's church and, as such, must remain deeply connected to that church in all that we do and all that we are. (For this last point, I must acknowledge the helpful critique of Mark Lau Branson, who says that he does not believe that individuals have vocation so much as the church has a vocation. He sees any individual's labor as an extension of the church's calling from God [personal communication]).

16. My thinking on giving, as will become clear, was profoundly shaped by a wonderful book by Thomas Jeavons and Rebekah Burch Basinger called *Growing Givers' Hearts* (San Francisco: Jossey-Bass, 2000). I need to acknowledge that debt up front because even the paragraphs that do not reference the book are indebted to its wisdom.

17. Brueggemann, "The Liturgy of Abundance, the Myth of Scarcity."

18. Robert Lynn makes an excellent point that should be noted here. He reminds us that every answer to the question, "Why give?" involves an appeal to some authority. This is a crucial point because pastors need to be aware when and how they use their authority. And they need to know that anytime they start talking about money, issues of authority are immediately on the table. Robert Wood Lynn, "Why Give?" in *Financing American Religion*, eds. Mark Chaves and Sharon Miller (Walnut Creek, Calif.: AltaMira Press, 1999), 55.

19. This is the thesis of Jeavons and Basinger in *Growing Givers' Hearts*. They believe that the purpose of giving is to grow the giver's heart.

Lightning Source UK Ltd.
Milton Keynes UK
UKHW02f1842260818

327839UK00016B/678/P

9 781620 328019